# Foul Deeds & Suspicious Deaths in Hampstead, Holborn & St Pancras

## *FOUL DEEDS AND SUSPICIOUS DEATHS* Series

Wharncliffe's *Foul Deeds and Suspicious Deaths* series explores, in detail, crimes of passion, brutal murders and foul misdemeanours from early modern times to the present day. Victorian street crime, mysterious deaths and modern murders tell tales where passion, jealousy and social depravation brought unexpected violence to those involved. From unexplained death and suicide to murder and manslaughter, the books provide a fascinating insight into the lives of both victims and perpetrators as well as society as a whole.

### Other titles in the series

Please contact us via any of the methods below for more information or a catalogue.
WHARNCLIFFE BOOKS
47 Church Street – Barnsley – South Yorkshire – S70 2AS
Tel: 01226 734555 – 734222 Fax: 01226 724438
E-mail: enquiries@pen-and-sword.co.uk -
Website: www.wharncliffebooks.co.uk

Foul Deeds & Suspicious Deaths in

# HAMPSTEAD, HOLBORN & ST PANCRAS

## MARK ASTON

*Series Editor*
**Brian Elliott**

**Wharncliffe Books**

**First Published in Great Britain in 2005 by**
**Wharncliffe Books**
*an imprint of*
**Pen and Sword Books Ltd.**
**47 Church Street**
**Barnsley**
**South Yorkshire**
**S70 2AS**

Copyright © Mark Aston 2005

ISBN: 1-903425-94-8

Typeset in 11/13pt Plantin by Mac Style Ltd, Scarborough.

Printed and bound in England by
CPI UK.

Pen and Sword Books Ltd incorporates the Imprints of
Pen & Sword Aviation, Pen & Sword Maritime,
Pen & Sword Military, Wharncliffe Books,
Pen & Sword Select, Pen and Sword Military Classics
and Leo Cooper.

For a complete list of Pen & Sword titles please contact
PEN & SWORD BOOKS LIMITED
47 Church Street
Barnsley
South Yorkshire
S70 2BR
England
E-mail: enquiries@pen-and-sword.co.uk
Website: www.pen-and-sword.co.uk

# Contents

# Introduction and Acknowledgements

Nothing grips the darker side of our imagination more than hearing grisly tales of past murder and malice. This book takes a journey back in time to a small, north-west corner of the nation's capital to recall a selection of gruesome events guaranteed to send a shiver down the spine of every reader.

The boroughs of Hampstead, Holborn and St Pancras amalgamated in 1965 to form the London Borough of Camden but each area still retains a unique identity, as well as a chilling past. Our trip down 'felony lane' will chronicle this past and, whilst it has not been possible to include every foul deed and suspicious death ever reported, an assortment of well-known and some not so well-known crimes spanning a period of three hundred and fifty years to 1955 is featured.

To the north lies Hampstead. With its open expanse of heath and roads into and out of the capital, the location was once the haunt of villainous highwaymen and footpads. To the south is Holborn, home to seventeenth-century coiners, fraudsters and a notorious public executioner who very nearly swung at the end of his own rope. Located between the two is St Pancras under whose administration north Bloomsbury, Camden Town, Kentish Town, Somers Town and King's Cross can be found. Each of these districts boasted criminal episodes equal to any found in fiction, such as cases involving death (allegedly) by witchcraft and the murders of the first Metropolitan Police officers. All these events and more are recounted, including duels to the death and gross miscarriages of justice, the latter equally as foul as any murder. New light too is shed on supposedly 'open and shut cases', leaving readers to decide for themselves about what really happened. Each crime reported is true and all persons documented are real. All, that is, with the exception of one rather curious 'anti-hero', whose somewhat eventful life is detailed in the first chapter. Again, it is left to the reader to decide whether such a character existed but no book covering suspicious deaths in St Pancras would be complete without mention of her unique story.

The realisation of this book would not have been possible without the help and support of a number of individuals. I would therefore like to thank my 'partners-in-crime' at Camden Local Studies and Archives Centre for their support during the research phase of this book. I'm sure they must have thought of planning a foul deed of their own to silence my endless 'did you know?' tales of local murder and intrigue!

Particular thanks must go to my colleagues Rachel Dilworth, whose 'pencilling wizardry' can be found throughout this publication, and to Richard Knight for giving full permission to allow extensive plundering of the Centre's illustration collection from where the vast majority of pictures featured are drawn, along with a number of photographs from the author's own camera or collection. Special thanks also to Matthew Greenland of the Press Association Picture Archive, John Dunne of the *Hampstead and Highgate Express*, John Richardson of the Camden History Society, and local author Brian Girling for kind permission to reproduce images from their collections or archives. Every attempt has been made to trace copyright holders. Apologies in advance to those concerned if an oversight has occurred. Any corrections will be included in any future editions of this book. Lastly, mention must be made of four excellent sources of information without which research into many of the foul deeds and suspicious deaths would have been a more arduous task, namely; the Old Bailey Proceedings Online, *The Times* Digital Archive 1785–1985, Mark Herber's *Criminal London* (2002) and the Heal Collection held at Camden Local Studies and Archives Centre.

# CHAPTER 1

# Mother Damnable: The Witch Queen of Kentish Town
## c.1600–80

*For her features were shrivelled and brown as a mummy's hide,*
*And she passed for a witch, whose amusement was homicide.*

Between 1563 and 1736 witchcraft was a capital offence in England. Throughout the seventeenth century, recorded accusations of the practice of witchcraft against individuals, especially against women, increased and the number of prosecutions in England rose sharply. Whilst superstition, ignorance and hysteria gripped much of the nation, Hampstead, Holborn and St Pancras remained relatively free of accusations, witch-hunts and prosecution except, that is, in the curious case of Mother Damnable, alias Mother Red Cap – the Witch Queen of Kentish Town:

*A cottage that stood between Kentish Town-road*
*And Parliament Hill, was the place of abode*
*Of that plague of North London – or rather "N.W"*
*With whose life and misdeeds you'll permit me to trouble you.*
*'Twas in Oliver's time, or in that of Queen Anne,*
*(It is not certain which,) that her doings began*
*To disturb the quiet folks. And it put them in dread*
*To catch sight of her head, in her cap of bright red:*
*For her features were shrivelled and brown as a mummy's hide,*
*And she passed for a witch, whose amusement was homicide.*[1]

Legend has it that the mere mention of Mother Damnable instilled fear and loathing into the minds of the residents of then rural Kentish Town: neighbouring Camden Town was yet to exist. Even as late as 1880, the story of Mother Damnable remained deeply rooted in Victorian romantic imagination, and homage continued to be paid in verse and prose, as the above example demonstrates. As for the true account of her life only Mother Damnable can verify but, of the many colourful stories, the following is perhaps the most commonly related version of her life.

Known also as Mother Red Cap, and in some contemporary texts as the 'Shrew of Kentish Town', Mother Damnable was born in the early

*Mother Damnable. A copy taken from an engraving published in 1793.*

seventeenth century. Her father, Jacob Bingham, a local brick maker, who later enlisted in the army, was posted to Scotland where he married a pedlar's daughter. They named their only child Jinney, who was only sixteen when she too gave birth. The father of the offspring was Jinney's boyfriend Coulter, alias 'Gypsy George'. Jacob Bingham built them a cottage on some wasteland near Kentish Town but, shortly after, tragedy occurred to upset this seemingly harmonious union. George was found guilty of sheep stealing in nearby Holloway and later hanged at Tyburn. A violent, hard drinking man called Darby replaced Gypsy George as Jinney's next love but his brutal treatment towards her led Jinney to seek help from her mother. The problem was instantly solved; Darby simply disappeared, leaving Jinney to pick up the pieces of another failed relationship.

Fate dealt Jinney a further blow when her parents were also removed from her life. Although the disappearance of Darby was never investigated, her parents were later accused and convicted of killing a woman with witchcraft. They too were hanged at Tyburn. Poor Jinney found comfort in the arms of her next lover, a man by the name of Pitcher, who moved into the cottage with her. Third time lucky in love for Jinney? Sadly not, for Pitcher's burnt remains were later discovered in Jinney's oven. By this time, Jinney had developed a wicked temper and poor Pitcher had resorted to hiding in the oven to seek sanctuary from her wrath. Jinney was tried but acquitted of his murder. A neighbour testified that Pitcher 'often got into the oven to hide himself from her tongue', suggesting that his death could have been accidental.

Jinney's reputation for ridding herself of partners became widespread. Now a recluse, and socially shunned by neighbours, only at nightfall did she venture out of her cottage in order to scavenge for food in nearby lanes and hedgerows. Shortly, her luck was to be given a temporary boost. A wealthy fugitive from the troubles of the Commonwealth offered her handsome sums of money in return for shelter. Despite reports of frequent quarrels, an understanding was established between the unlikely partners, with the political runaway eventually staying with her for some time. It was also during the Cromwellian period that her cottage was reported to have been used by 'Moll Cut-purse', the infamous highway woman, as a refuge from authority. Nevertheless, trouble was never far away and the untimely death of her lodger re-ignited old suspicions and accusations. Jinney was rumoured to have poisoned him, using witchcraft to bring about his downfall. The ensuing inquest proved nothing and, although lonely once more, she was now financially comfortable.

This episode, along with her increasing eccentricity, caused Jinney to become even more reviled. Baited and taunted by locals, she in return would scream profanities at all who passed her gate. Residents would often gather outside her cottage, blaming her for local misfortune. Jinney later became known as 'Mother Red Cap' due to her distinctive red headwear. Looking the part, with a large black cat permanently at her side, she was now reputed to be a witch, fortune-teller and healer of strange diseases. Samuel Palmer, in his *History of St Pancras*, describes her as possessing,

> *a large broad nose, heavy shaggy eyebrows, sunken eyes, and lank and leathern cheeks; her forehead wrinkled, her mouth wide and her looks sullen and unmoved. On her shoulders was thrown a dark grey frieze, with black patches, which looked at a distance like flying bats.*[2]

Perhaps the most amusing but purely fictitious episode to emerge from Victorian desire to resurrect and re-establish the Mother Red Cap tale was published in 1843.[3] This account purports to have been written by Henry Foxhall of Whitehall in 1666 to an associate, Mr Charles Firebrace. On a journey with friends, including Lord Rochester, to visit Lord Wotton in Belsize Park, Foxhall recounts a chance meeting with Mother Red Cap:

> *We proceeded over very rough roads towards Hampstead, when, on coming to that part of the road which leads towards Kentish Town,* [today, the junction where Camden High Street converges with Kentish Town Road in Camden Town] *we saw an array of people opposite a small thatched dwelling, and enquiring the cause, a butcher's boy told us that they were baiting 'Old Mother Red Cap'.*

Foxhall then provides account of how Lord Rochester jumps from their carriage to meet with Jinney and, after a duel of words, rejoins his friends vowing to return later that night to sneak into the witch's cottage disguised as the devil, complete with horns and forked tail. Fuelled by an evening of drinking, and dressed as 'his Satanic Majesty', Rochester duly entered the cottage and found its resident transfixed, as if in a trance like state, later remarking:

> *I looked at the beldame, but there was no motion, no change of countenance, her eyes remained fixed upon me. Then threatening her with a thrust of my horns and exhibiting my claws, I wisked my tail over and around her, crying, 'fire and brimestone', and left her.*

Presumably the object of this drunken lark was to provide self-amusement but his jape seemed to have backfired, leaving the ridiculous Rochester to exit the premises with his forked tail firmly between his legs.

Even her death one night was as dramatic an event as anything that had preceded her in life. Evidently, hundreds of onlookers witnessed the 'real' Satan enter Mother Red Cap's cottage that fateful evening, never to re-emerge. The old crone was found dead in the morning, sitting in front of her fireplace, holding a crutch over it, and from this was suspended a teapot containing a noxious brew of herbs, drugs and liquid. Some of this concoction was later fed to her cat, which died soon after. Furthermore, it was said that an undertaker had to break Jinney's rigoured limbs in order to fit her into her coffin before being buried at midnight under a local tree. The case was referred to the coroner but no verdict as to the real cause of her passing was reached.

As with many engaging stories, Jinney was to be immortalised long after her death. For nearly three hundred years, her moniker of Mother Red Cap was used as the name of a public house that stood on the supposed site of her cottage. With Camden Town to eventually develop around the environs of the pub, the *Mother Red Cap* was occasionally referred to as 'the half way house to Hampstead and Highgate', an important landmark for those travelling between London and the

*The old* Mother Red Cap *public house, 1746.*

north. Meanwhile, debate amongst local historians is divided as to the exact origins of the pub's name. Some argue that the cottage later became a tavern owned by another red cap wearing lady. She was said to have possessed a much friendlier disposition than Jinney. This Mother Red Cap had been a camp follower in the Duke of Marlborough's armies and, after the peace of Utrecht in 1713, set up a hedge alehouse/roadside inn. Others argue that the pub had been in existence longer. Evidence was once presented in the form of a coin or token found dated 1667 bearing the inscription 'Mother Read Capp in Holl[o]way'. Thus, giving credence to the argument that it was indeed named after Jinney. It was only in 1986 that the thrice re-built *Mother Red Cap* changed its name to the *World's End*.

Therefore, if ever quenching your thirst in the pub today, think back three centuries to Jinney Bingham, 'For her features were shrivelled and brown as a mummy's hide, And she passed for a witch, whose amusement was homicide.' Did she indeed exist at all as thus described? If so, was her life shaped by a series of tragic events and failed relationships in her youth that led her to murder? Or, was her life pre-determined by supernatural forces that already dictated that she would become Mother Damnable – Witch Queen of Kentish Town? Only Jinney will ever know the truth!

# CHAPTER 2

# Gentlemen of the Road: Highway Robbery 1669–1725

*His corpse hung in an iron framework and remained there for eighteen years as a chilling warning to others …*

The first mounted highwaymen were Royalist officers who took to the road when they became outlaws under the Commonwealth. Many were considered heroes because they robbed the wealthy but, in reality, they were desperate criminals and any traveller with full pockets was fair game. Hampstead, with its secluded country roads and heath, ideal for escape and concealment, and close proximity to the capital, made for a particularly irresistible centre of operations for these 'equestrian pirates'.

One of the area's earliest and most famous highwaymen was not a refugee from the Civil War but a Frenchman. Claude Duval (or Du Vall) hailed from Domfront, Normandy, and travelled to England after the Restoration with the household of the Duke of Richmond. By the late 1660s, presumably finding the glamour and profit of life on the road infinitely more preferable than domestic servitude, Duval discovered that Hampstead and its heath offered an excellent opportunity to relieve the wealthy of their goods. The Norman found the route between Golders Hill and Fortune Green particularly profitable, so much so that the road between these two locations became known as Duval's Lane. Today, Platt's Lane marks the route. Folklore alleges that, having held a carriage to ransom on Hampstead Hill, Duval danced a moonlit minuet with a lady passenger whilst her male companion lay bound after the robbery. His career as a highwayman, however, was very brief. A proclamation, dated 19 November 1669, of a reward of £20 for the arrest of 'Lewis, alias Lodowick, alias Claude Deval, alias Brown' seems to have paid dividend. He was captured when the worse for drink in the *Hole-in-the-Wall* tavern in Chandos Street (now Place), Covent Garden. Aged only twenty-six, Duval was tried on Monday, 17 January 1670 and hanged four days later at Tyburn. A mourning coach respectfully conveyed his body to the *Tangier* tavern, St Giles, where it lay in state until interment. An epitaph over his grave in the old St Paul's Church, Covent Garden, was said to have included the following lines:

*A copy of a popular engraving showing 'dandy' highwayman Claude Duval inviting a female victim to dance a moonlight minuet on Hampstead Hill.*

> *Here lies Du Vall: Reader, if male thou art,*
> *Look to thy purse; if female, to thy heart.*
> *Much havoc hath he made of both; for all*
> *Men he made stand, and women he made fall.*[4]

In stark contrast to the dashing Duval were Francis Jackson and his four-strong gang, comprising of James Slater, Walter Parkhurst, John White and John Williams. All were labourers turned highwayman from Bedfont, Middlesex, who menaced the heaths and commons of north and west London. In 1674, they committed a series of robberies, and of particular consequence was the holding up of two coaches, one near Hounslow Heath on 16 March and the other near Staines two days later. After a six-mile chase, following the first hold up, Jackson and the gang evaded escape but, following the Staines robbery, the highwaymen made it cross-country to Harrow only to be confronted by fifty men equipped with guns, pitchforks and other assorted weaponry. A chase ensued and the gang fled south to Paddington, finally ending up at Hampstead Heath (near North End), where another party of armed men laid in wait. Amidst fierce fighting, Francis Jackson killed one of the Hampstead men, Henry Miller, by running him through with a sword. But, before long, the battle was lost and the gang captured alive.

Following a signed confession, known as *Jackson's Recantations*, and dated 14 April 1674, all except James Slater were convicted of an assortment of crimes, including murder, and duly executed. Although captured, Slater died in Newgate Prison on 8 April before he could be brought to trial. After execution, the body of Francis Jackson was gibbeted near to the scene of the crime at North End, Hampstead. His corpse hung in an iron framework and remained there for eighteen years as a chilling warning to deter others from a life of wrongdoing. The gibbet was erected between two trees, the Gibbet Elms, one of which survived until 1907 when it was blown down in a gale. A verse from the *Triennial Mayor* published in 1691 recalls the grisly site:

*As often upon Hampstead Heath,*
*Have seen a felon long since put to death,*
*Hang crackling in the sun his parchment skin*
*Which to his ear had shrivell'd up his chin.*[5]

*The Gibbet Elms, North End, Hampstead, from a drawing by T Hastings, 1819.*

The story of Francis Jackson and his association with Hampstead is well and accurately documented, unlike the varied but unsubstantiated accounts of infamous Richard 'Dick' Turpin (*d*.1737). Turpin has long been connected with Hampstead Heath and, in particular, with the *Spaniards Inn* situated to the north of this famous open space. Tradition has it that the pub's landlord is said to have given the highwayman spare keys to the stables and the adjoining tollgate for rapid escape should danger beckon. Subterranean passages from the Spaniards were also said to have extended under the Heath and used as an alternative access route for the robber. Even so, his connection with Hampstead remains unproven, especially given that the pub was unlikely to have existed during Turpin's lifetime.

In spite of the fate that befell Jackson and associates, the end of the seventeenth century witnessed a near epidemic of highwaymen operating in Hampstead and nearby Highgate. So much so that, in September 1699, the Duke of Ormond's troopers were ordered to scour the roads nightly from Islington to Hampstead and Highgate. How effective these nocturnal patrols proved is unknown but the mounted robbers were not the only menace travellers and the authorities faced. The highwaymen's 'pedestrian cousins-in-crime', the notorious footpads, were less glamorous but no less dangerous. Trees and hedgerows lined many of the roads in rural north London and, as such, proved to be perfect hunting grounds for local footpads. In particular, the routes that took travellers north via Kentish Town to Hampstead and Highgate, such as Hampstead Road, Gray's Inn Lane and Fig Lane (now Crowndale Road), were often where rich pickings could be found. These violent criminals knew that, if apprehended and found guilty, they would be executed or given life sentences and therefore did not hesitate to kill in order to escape or prevent their prey identifying them later.

Throughout this seemingly criminally prolific era, the *Proceedings of the Old Bailey* record countless trials at the Old Bailey Sessions House involving footpads accused of robbery in Hampstead, Holborn and St Pancras. Some footpads worked alone attacking unsuspecting revellers returning from a night at the local tavern, whilst others hunted in gangs ready to rob lone riders or carriages. Moonless nights were particularly favourable, as robbers could spring unseen into action. Ill-gotten gains were usually fenced through an underground network of contacts. Nevertheless, whilst profit could be high, an evening's work could also yield very little or, if caught, worse – a one-way trip to the gallows!

Take the case of two resident St Pancras robbers, John Morphew and Nathaniel Jackson. For the assault and robbery of Richard Dennis, on

*Exposed to the elements: The Old Sessions House in Old Bailey, c.1720. The building was remodelled and enclosed in 1737 and rebuilt in 1774.*

20 June 1722, both were hanged a few weeks later for their troubles. With an accomplice, who was to escape justice on this occasion, Morphew and Jackson attacked the unfortunate Dennis at gunpoint midway between Tottenham Court Road and Hampstead. One could possibly understand the gang's motivation for robbery if the end result justified the means, but the haul included just a small amount of clothing, six lemons and five ounces of human hair![6] Morphew and Jackson followed a fellow St Pancratian to the gallows who, a year or so earlier, had set his sights on more lucrative bounty. On the night of 20 February 1721, William Barton chanced upon the carriage of John, Lord Viscount Lisbon and his pregnant wife returning to London from Hampstead. Barton and two cohorts, Dickinson and Reading, stopped the aristocratic coach and relieved its owner of a silver hilted sword worth £6 and about 12 shillings in silver. Lord Lisbon attempted to fight back by raising his cane to Reading who, in evidence, 'clapt a

Pistol to my Lord's Breast and threatned to shoot him' and then admitted taking 'a Snuff-Box from my Lady; that my Lord pray'd us not to take her Wedding Ring, she being with Child, and he this Evidence promised they would not.' In allowing Lady Lisbon to keep her ring, this glimmer of humanity perhaps saved James Reading from the noose, as only Barton was indicted and found guilty of theft with violence. Whether Reading was excused prosecution in return for his betrayal of his partner-in-crime is not known but, for the inconvenience caused to Lord and Lady Lisbon, pitiful William Barton went on to receive full, uncompromising eighteenth-century retribution at the end of a rope.[7]

The same punishment was meted out less than two years later to Matthew Flood, John Levee, and Richard Oakey following a ruthless crime wave perpetrated by the three throughout Hampstead, Holborn and St Pancras. On 16 January 1723, each stood indicted at the Old Bailey Sessions charged with theft with violence, robbery and theft with violence, and highway robbery.[8] Their case involved three separate incidents, one of which featured notorious thief-taker Jonathan Wild. Simeon Betts was the first victim set upon by the three men on 26 November 1722. Dragged along notorious Fig Lane by the trio and into a field near St Pancras (Old) Church, the helpless and beaten Betts was relieved of two guineas in cash and a two-shilling muslin turnover. These dangerous wretches evidently worked up an appetite after the robbery as they later shared their ill-gotten gains whilst enjoying half a goose in a nearby eatery. For their next outing, a few hours after dusk on 10 December, Flood and his cohorts headed north to Hampstead. Colonel Cope and William Young were to be the next unfortunates to fall prey to the gang. A veritable treasure trove amounting to over £35 was stolen from the travelling companions, including a gold watch alone worth £30, a gold chain valued at £4 and a ring costing 15 shillings. A few days later, on 14 December, the three this time headed south to Holborn. Here, James Forey was relieved of a dimity gown and petticoat worth 30 shillings, as well as other goods.

Meanwhile, incensed by their loss in Hampstead, Cope and Young hired the services of Jonathan Wild, Thief-taker General, to bring the gang to justice. Swinging into action, Wild offered a handsome reward of £10 to anyone with information that lead to the arrest of the trio. With little honour amongst the criminal fraternity, information quickly arrived and Wild was able to apprehend his men. At their trial, Flood, Levee and Oakey all denied the accusations levelled at them by the thief-taker and 'inveigh'd bitterly against Jonathan Wild, calling him opprobrious Names, but had nothing to say in their Defence.' Needless to say, the three were found guilty as charged and each was given the punishment of death by hanging. These miscreants and countless other ne'er-do-wells were, however, to enjoy a posthumous last laugh on their captor. For only two years later Wild also found himself swinging from Tyburn's gallows, with the burial ground of St Pancras (Old) Church near Fig Lane designated his final resting place.

*'Thief-taker General' Jonathan Wild (c.1682–1725).*

The thief-taker in fact led a double life. The so-called respectable side of Wild saw him recover stolen goods and bring many violent criminals to justice but his alter ego shared many of the traits of those he sent to Tyburn. He worked with highwaymen and burglars, receiving stolen goods, whilst simultaneously controlling a network of informants. Wild even protected criminals from prosecution by bribing court officials or paying people for false testimony. Despite his value as thief-taker, he was eventually arrested on 15 February 1725. In revenge for having been slighted by Wild, a thief named Edwards made public the thief-taker's role in helping a known highwayman escape from a constable. For this and other offences, Jonathan Wild was found guilty and sentenced to hang at Tyburn on 24 May 1725. He was not, alas, destined to then rest in peace. St Pancras (Old) Church was the scene of Wild's third marriage to Mary Dean in 1721, and its burial ground was, for a very short time, his home in death: the burial register records him simply as 'J.W'. A few nights after his interment, a hearse and six horses were seen waiting suspiciously at the corner of Fig Lane near to the burial ground. Later, his empty coffin was found in place of the cortège. This was probably the work of body snatchers who doubtless thought his body a prize specimen for surgical dissection. Justice indeed for a thief-taker who himself was taken thief for unashamedly operating on both sides of the law!

# CHAPTER 3

# Body on the Hill: The Assassination of Sir Edmund Berry Godfrey
## 1678

*... strangled and impaled on his own sword.*

One of England's most enduring criminal mysteries has been the murder of Sir Edmund Berry Godfrey, Justice of the Peace for Westminster and Middlesex, in 1678. Sir Edmund's murdered body was found on Primrose Hill (then part of St Pancras Parish) on Thursday, 17 October that year; he had been strangled and impaled on his own sword. The true identity of his killer(s) has yet to be revealed.

The dead body of fifty-six-year-old Sir Edmund had been found in a ditch on the south side of the Hill, about two fields from the White House, later the *Chalk Farm* tavern. It was removed to the house where it remained on view to onlookers for two days. Bishop Burnett was one who inspected the dead knight's body shortly after its discovery. He noted that,

[Godfrey's] *sword was thrust through him; but no blood was on his clothes or about him. His shoes were clean. His money was in his pocket, but nothing was about his neck, and a mark was round it about an inch broad, which showed how he was strangled. His breast was likewise all over marked with bruises, and his neck was broken. There were many drops of white waxlights on his breeches, which he never used himself;*

*Sir Edmund Berry Godfrey (1622–78).*

*and since only persons of quality and priests use those lights, this made conclude in whose hands he must have been.*

The Bishop was unquestionably alluding to a Catholic plot to topple Charles II, the investigation of which Sir Edmund was to play a central but perilous role.

Another inextricably linked with this affair was clergyman Titus Oates. During the summer of 1678, Reverend Oates offered information about a Catholic conspiracy known as the 'Popish Plot'. The alleged plan was to replace an assassinated Charles II with his Catholic brother, James. Sir Edmund was selected to examine the allegations and, as such, worked closely with Oates. He took the clergyman's depositions, denouncing the Catholics, as being wholly reliable. Shortly after his review of the evidence, Godfrey believed himself also to be in danger from Catholics who sought to stop his enquiry into their plotting. His fears as to his own safety were to be well founded. The last time the knight was seen alive was about 1 pm on 12 October, after which he simply disappeared. His body was eventually discovered five days later, head downwards in the aforementioned ditch. As robbery played no part in the crime, the perpetrators of his death had perhaps wished to give the impression that Sir Edmund had committed suicide. There was no history of him ever displaying suicidal tendencies and, besides, would a man in the act of killing himself be able to thrust his sword completely through his own body so that it emerged out of his back 'for the length of two hand-breaths?' Also, this didn't take into consideration the fact that there was no blood on his clothes that such a sword thrust would cause and, furthermore, suicide doesn't explain the strangulation marks found around his neck. The placing of the sword was either a pitiable attempt to imply suicide or, more so, a final damming statement from his murderer(s). To many, his death seemed to confirm their fear that there was indeed a conspiracy to reinstate a Catholic monarch. This fear had its part to play following the inquest into Sir Edmund's death.

At the inquest, the jury returned a verdict of strangling by some person or persons unknown but it was not long before direct accusations aimed at Catholics surfaced. At first, a man named William Bedloe alleged that Sir Edmund had been murdered at Somerset House. He asserted that a Jesuit priest, Le Fevre, along with two accomplices, had smothered the justice between two pillows and that he (Bedloe) had been offered £2,000 to dispose of the body. Unfortunately, his story didn't match the facts of the case, so he modified it and pointed the finger of accusation at a Catholic silversmith named Miles Prance. Prance was tortured into confession but later recanted, naming three Somerset House staff as the would-be assassins, namely Robert Green, Lawrence Hill and Henry Berry (a Protestant), all of whom worked in the Queen's Catholic Chapel at Somerset House. Such were the loose methods of accepting evidence that prevailed during the period that Prance was allowed to be the chief accuser. There now appeared two versions from the silversmith on how Sir Edmund lost his life. The first bears witness to the justice

*The murder of Sir Edmund Berry Godfrey by supposed Roman Catholic assassins.*

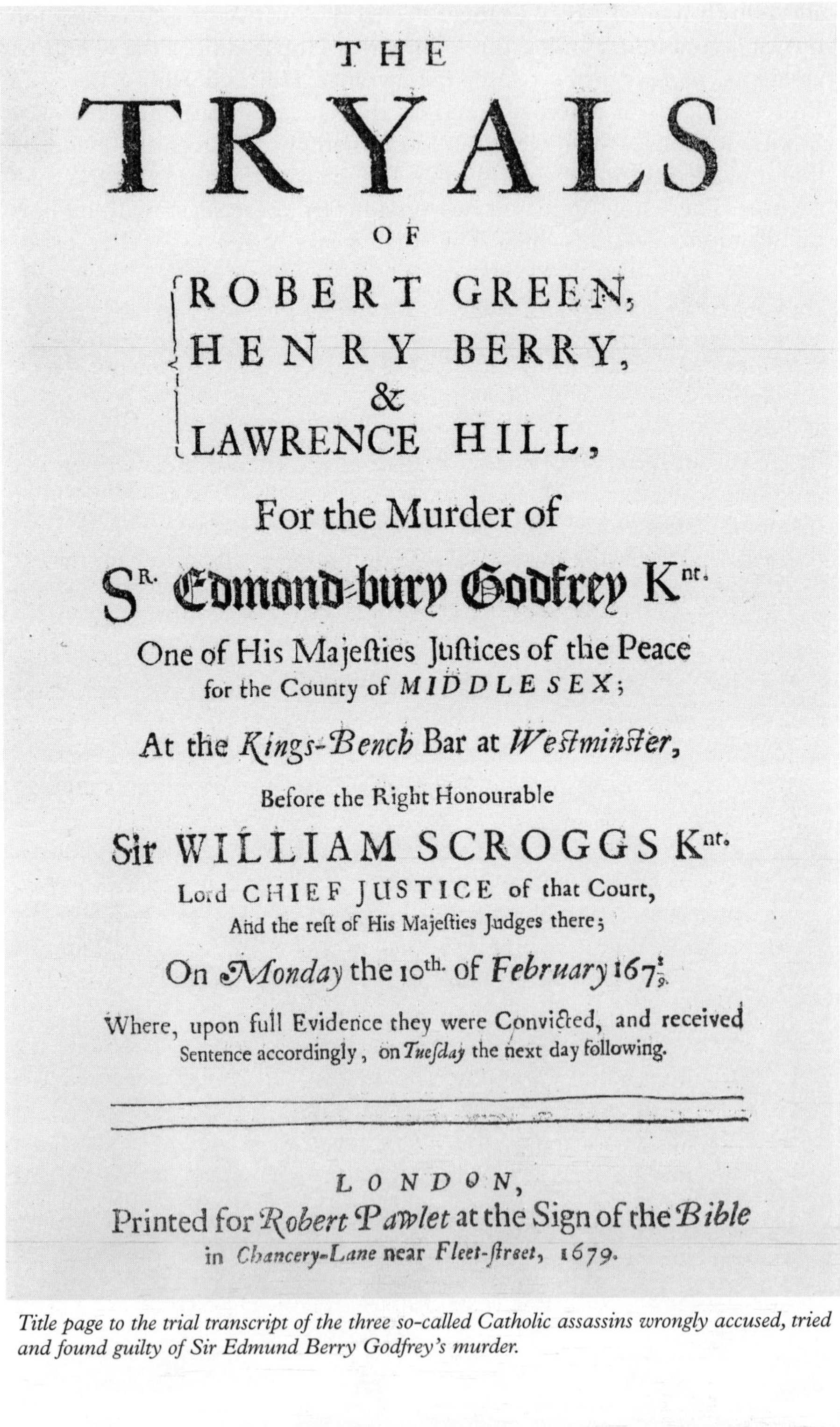

# THE
# TRYALS

OF

{ROBERT GREEN,
HENRY BERRY,
&
LAWRENCE HILL,

For the Murder of

Sᴿ **Edmond-bury Godfrey** Kⁿᵗ·

One of His Majesties Justices of the Peace
for the County of *MIDDLESEX;*

At the *Kings-Bench* Bar at *Westminster,*

Before the Right Honourable

## Sir WILLIAM SCROGGS Kⁿᵗ·

Lord CHIEF JUSTICE of that Court,
And the rest of His Majesties Judges there;

On *Monday* the 10ᵗʰ· of *February* 167⅞.

Where, upon full Evidence they were Convicted, and received
Sentence accordingly, on *Tuesday* the next day following.

----

LONDON,
Printed for *Robert Pawlet* at the Sign of the *Bible*
in *Chancery-Lane* near *Fleet-street,* 1679.

*Title page to the trial transcript of the three so-called Catholic assassins wrongly accused, tried and found guilty of Sir Edmund Berry Godfrey's murder.*

attempting to separate two servants that he had caught fighting in the yard of Somerset House. Prance alleged that, during the scuffle, Robert Green approached Sir Edmund and proceeded to strangle him:

> *When Sir Edmundbury Godfrey came down to the bench, Greene, who followed him, put about his neck a large twisted handkerchief: and thereupon all the rest assisted, and dragged him into a corner ... Greene ... thumped him on the breast and twisted his neck until he broke it ... but his body remained warm, and seemed hardly dead ... After keeping the body concealed for four days they put it in a sedan-chair, and about midnight took it to a house in Soho, whence the corpse was ultimately carried by Hill, on horseback, to the spot on Primrose Hill where it was afterwards found, and there they thrust the knight's sword through his body.*

In the second version of events, Prance offers a variation claiming that the three accused, with help from two Irish priests named Girald (or Fitzgerald) and Kelly, had simply strangled Sir Godfrey and then stabbed him with his own sword. Then, after keeping the murdered body concealed for a few days, the assassins threw it into a ditch on Primrose Hill.

In the circumstances, either version would probably been acceptable as, on 10 February 1679 at the Old Bailey Sessions, the Somerset House trio were tried for the murder of Sir Edmund. Presided over by Lord Chief Justice Scroggs and George Jeffries, the Recorder of London, the trial was heavily weighted against the defendants and, in spite of the many discrepancies in the evidence and the strong denials by the accused, the three men were found guilty and sent to the gallows. The verdict was a foregone conclusion. Here, during a period when the bearing of false witness was all too commonplace, the evidence was clearly manufactured. So, in order to allay fears of regicide and a return to Catholicism, these three Catholics had to be burdened with the crime.

Green and Hill swung at Tyburn on 21 February 1679, and Berry followed a week later. After their deaths, much doubt shadowed the trio's guilt, with many viewing their trial as a major miscarriage of justice. As for Titus Oates, the instigator of the chain of events, he eventually paid the price for his lies about the Catholic plots. Convicted of perjury, the clergyman was to be whipped and placed in the pillory on five days of each year for the rest of his life. Due to being nearly killed by the mob at his first pillory, Oates' sentence was replaced with another whipping and three years imprisonment. He died in 1705 aged fifty-seven.

Meanwhile, the ongoing debate surrounding the Godfrey case has brought forth many theories. Some were convinced that the Catholics were indeed guilty of the crime, whilst others believed that associates of Titus Oates committed the murder in order to reinforce the growing belief in a Popish plot. Even the idea of suicide was re-considered, despite the overwhelming physical evidence to suggest the contrary. For over three hundred years now the mystery behind Sir Edmund Berry Godfrey's death has confounded historians and undoubtedly will continue to do so for centuries to come.

*Clergyman Titus Oates seen here in the pillory following his conviction for perjury.*

# CHAPTER 4

# A Miscellany of Murder and Misdemeanour in the Eighteenth Century
## 1717–86

*On occasion, the guilty persons were sentenced to swing close to where the foul deed was committed before being transported to Surgeons' Hall.*

This chapter highlights some of the foul deeds and crimes that have taken place in Hampstead, Holborn and St Pancras during the eighteenth century. Then, as still today, crimes of passion and drunken assault were commonplace. Theft, burglary and forgery were also mainstay activities of the eighteenth-century professional criminal. Unlike modern times, however, punishment for those found guilty was swift and severe; no short-term custodial sentences or community service for our ancestor villains. Instead, hanging, life imprisonment or transportation were amongst a variety of penalties available to the judiciary when passing sentence. Such were the rigours of life two to three hundred years ago that even these harsh punishments proved no deterrent to those who chose to murder and misdemean.

## Part one: Wilful murder

Little did seventeen-year-old Thomas Wilford realise that, when after being hanged for murdering his wife, he was destined to be the first executee in England to have the dubious honour of being posthumously delivered to Surgeons' Hall for dissection.[9] On Monday, 28 May 1752, Thomas and his twenty-two-year-old wife, Sarah Williams, were married in a location near Fleet Lane. The happy couple were to live under the roof of landlord John Undershill in Dyot[t] Street, Bloomsbury. Nonetheless, their marital bliss was to come to an abrupt end only a week later. During the early hours of the following Monday, a fellow lodger sharing the same floor as the couple burst into the landlord's room and, waking him, announced that Wilford had killed his wife. Upon investigating the claim, Undershill saw that the young bridegroom was covered in blood:

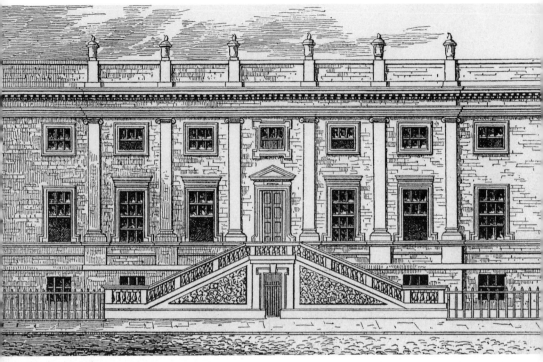

*Surgeons' Hall, Old Bailey, 1800.*

*I saw the blood run off his arm to his breeches; he was bloody as high as his elbow ... her throat was cut, her head almost off, and a bloody knife was lying in the window. She was quite dead, dressed all but her bodice, cap and apron.*

Alerted to the scene by John Undershill, Constable Henry Cooling found confession from the blood drenched Wilford easily forthcoming, 'he [Wilford] told me that he had killed his wife; that he would willingly die for her. He told me the knife was in the window in the same room.' What went on between the newly weds was never discovered – an early marital tiff that had spiralled out of control? Or, perhaps, the young man harboured an insane jealousy of his wife and had attacked her after hearing of a clandestine flirtation. Undershill later testified that Wilford said that if he could not marry Sarah he would go crazy – evidence, this time, of an unsound mind? Even at his trial on 25 June 1752, Thomas Wilford simply informed the Old Bailey jury that 'he had nothing to say.' A new act passed a few months earlier 'for better preventing the horrid crime of murder' stipulated that those found guilty of murder after its enactment were to be hanged, as usual, but then should have his or her body delivered to Surgeons' Hall to be dissected and anatomised. Young Thomas Wilford was to be its first candidate. By introducing further humiliation after execution, it was hoped that this addition punishment would be further deterrent to those contemplating taking another's life. But, in the years following this new act, the desired effect proved ineffectual and north-west London continued to witness murder in all its variant forms.

*John Rocque's Map of London, published in 1746, showing the* Mother Red Cap *public house and Fig Lane (now Crowndale Road).*

After being in force for almost twenty-years, this supposed deterrent did little to abate the murderous resolve of one Richard Hewett. On 10 April 1771, Hewett and accomplice, Benjamin Johnson, appeared on trial at the Old Bailey Sessions indicted with the wilful murder of Sarah Orbell in Fig Lane, St Pancras.[10] Hewett stood accused of,

> giving her several mortal blows and bruises on the head, breast and stomach. &c. of which she instantly died; and the other [Johnson] for being present, aiding, abetting, comforting, assisting, and maintaining him, the said murder to do and commit.

During the afternoon of Thursday, 7 February 1771, whilst drinking at the *Goat* alehouse in Charing Cross, Hewett and Johnson, both Hackney coachmen, invited Sarah Orbell and her friend Mary Smith to dine with them at the *Mother Red Cap* public house, today the site of the *World's End* pub, Camden Town. With Hewett transporting Orbell in his coach and Smith riding with Johnson, the four made their way north to the hostelry, not before stopping in at least two pubs on the way. Smith remembers alighting briefly at the *Coach and Horses* in Holborn in which '[we] had a pot of brandy-hot; one of the prisoners paid for it.' The party finally arrived at the *Mother Red Cap* at about 4 pm, where they enjoyed

*At Mother Red Caps on the road to Hampstead by Samuel Hieronymous Grimm, 1772. Seen here is the road south that, a year earlier, took Sarah Orbell to her death after an afternoon's socialising with friends.*

a meal of cold roast beef, bread and cheese and all washed down with a pot of beer and yet more brandy. According to Mary Smith, a great time was had 'laughing and joking and agreeable altogether', but little did she realise that mirth would soon turn to murder!

All four revellers left the Red Cap at about 7 pm, and here Smith attests that she and Orbell were not 'fuddled' despite the copious amounts of liquor they had each consumed since late morning. Once again, Hewett and Sarah travelled together, with Johnson and Mary following. After a short while, the two coaches headed east along Fig Lane (now Crowndale Road). Approximately one hundred yards ahead of Johnson's vehicle, Hewett suddenly stopped. Mary Smith then witnessed her friend fall from the coach, get up and attempt to run off. The coachman jumped down, caught her, and according to Mary,

*pulled her about, and dragged her upon the ground by her legs; she was holding her petticoats down with one hand, and with the other she catched hold of a little stump; he pulled at her, but could not get any further; he let her go, and then I [Mary] ran away: I was much frightened. When I left her, she lay long the ground, upon her back, and Hewett stood close by.*

The deed done, Mary ran to the turnpike at Battle Bridge (later King's Cross) but never saw or heard from her friend or Hewett again. Mary Smith did not seek assistance for her friend, as she thought that Sarah would get away from the clutches of her aggressor. Sarah's body was discovered shortly after the attack by a passer-by, Joseph Martin. He initially believed Sarah to be intoxicated but upon closer inspection, and having lifted her lifeless arm, feared the worst. Waving down both a passing coal cart and a broad wheeled wagon, Martin invited one of the drivers to assist him to further evaluate his discovery. The driver observed that the body had 'a bruise on the side of her temples ... [and] ... when we went to move her she bled very fast from her nose, mouth and ears.' The corpse was carried to the nearby *Crown* public house where, two days later, it was medically examined by John Jones. He later recounted his findings:

*First I examined her head before she was stripped; her right jaw was broke; it was on Saturday, the day but one after this murder was committed; just behind her right ear her skull was broke and pushed in; there was a scratch upon her left temple, as if done against the ground.*

In his defence, Richard Hewett stated that 'after the deceased got out of my coach I shut the door up, and saw no more of her. I went down

Tottenham Court Road: she was very much in liquor. I went directly home.' Johnson's defence was presented in an equally matter of fact way, 'as soon as this woman [Mary Smith] that is here got out of my coach I drove away; I did not see her nor Hewett any more.' Hewett called no fewer that nineteen people to give character statement, each extolling his many virtues; 'I do not believe he would hurt a worm ... a man of remarkable disposition ... he is a very honest, sober man ... not given to quarrel ... I could trust my life in his hands ... [etc].' In spite of his friends testifying upon oath that he was a paragon of sobrietious respectably, the jury found him guilty. Was it just a case of the demon drink getting the better of his good-natured side or did Hewett harbour a murderous, dark side little seen by his associates? The prisoner received sentence immediately. He was to be executed and afterwards his body dissected and anatomised. Meanwhile, Benjamin Johnson was acquitted of all charges. An interesting addendum to the case saw the prosecution expenses borne by St Pancras ratepayers. A meeting of the local vestry on 2 April 1771 agreed that monies would be available from the parish poor rate to cover legal fees; a clear sign that the authority was prepared to take direct action to tackle crimes of this nature.

Not satisfied with simply hanging murderers at Tyburn before dissection, an additional 'shame' was often added to a death sentence. On occasion, the guilty persons were sentenced to swing close to where the foul deed was committed before being transported to Surgeons' Hall. Such was the fate that befell our next set of killers in 1786.

A mile or so north from where Sarah Orbell met her fate fifteen-years earlier, a murderous tragedy shook the small, rural community of Kentish Town. The crime centred on three figures. These were Walter Horseman, cowkeeper and milkman, his wife Mary, and an ex-servant, eighteen-year-old Joseph Rickards. In a similar case to that concerning teenage killer, Thomas Wilford, this too was a crime of passion, although this time a motive was apparent. Bedfordshire-born Rickards had been in the employ of Walter Horseman at his dairy in Kentish Town Road for about eighteen months when, in early January 1786, he was dismissed for evidently not doing his work. This did not deter Rickards from returning to Horseman's house on numerous occasions following his dismissal. Mary Horseman admitted to feeding him on several repeat visits, explaining that the young Rickards had not worked since leaving her husband's employ.

The cowkeeper's wife may well have regretted playing host to a hungry Joseph Rickards had she known the fate that was to befall her husband a month later, during the early hours of 11 February. Mary later explained that she and her husband were not sleeping together. As

*Horseman's Dairy, Kentish Town in 1788. Two years earlier, and blinded by love, seventeen-year-old Joseph Rickards killed his master, Walter Horseman. Young Joseph was later hanged in a field opposite the dairy, after which his body was taken to Surgeons' Hall for dissection.*

their fourteen-month-old child was teething quite badly, Mary elected to sleep in a lower floor room and this arrangement prevented her husband's slumbers from being disturbed. The couple's four-year-old daughter slept upstairs with her father and it was she that cried out that something was amiss. Her cry alerted her ten-year-old brother sleeping in an adjoining room and, in turn, he woke his mother, informing her that his father urgently wanted to see her. The scene that greeted Mary Horseman was alarming:

> *I went in directly, and by the light of the moon, he seemed to be quite black with blood from his face to his waist, the moon shone very bright, and there are two large windows in the room, he was sitting up in the bed, and as far as his waist appeared black and covered with blood. When I saw him, I said, Horseman, my dear creature, what is the matter with you? he said to me, Lord bless you! something has run over my face; I said, Lord bless you*

*child! run over your face! why you are nothing but blood; he made me answer, have you got a candle? I said, no child, I did not wait for a candle: I went down immediately, and got a candle, and when I came up, I found him beat and cut all to pieces; his forehead, and his eyes and nose were cut all to pieces; I asked him to tell me how it came, and he said I do not know, do not ask me, I do not know how it came. I called Trotman up, to go and fetch his nephew to me, and likewise to order the doctor and surgeons to come, that live at Kentish Town, then I went and got the pillow case off the pillow to wrap round his head, to try to stop the blood, then I got him to lay down in the bed.*

A day after the incident, Mr Heavyside, a surgeon, arrived to examine Walter Horseman but he found the victim's skull 'so mangled, that there was no possibility for any art to assist him.' The murder weapon was discovered to have been an iron bar. This had inflicted a mortal wound some three inches in length, two inches deep and one inch wide and was later found at the scene of crime. Poor Horseman didn't die instantly but miraculously held onto life for just over a week, finally succumbing to his wounds on 19 February. Although suspicion for the attack fell upon Joseph Rickards, no one had actually witnessed him being in the house at the time of the assault. The attacker, someone who obviously had an intimate knowledge of the interior of the Horseman residence, had stole in, attacked the sleeping victim and then made an anonymous getaway. Perhaps Rickards thought that he had got away with the crime, as he confidently remained in Kentish Town for the ensuing period. He had even been taken by the headborough of the parish of St Pancras to visit and shake the hand of his injured, former master. After this, he still strenuously denied any part in the attack but, following the inevitable death of the cowkeeper, Rickards' luck finally expired. He was apprehended only a few doors from Horseman's dairy in the *Anglers* public house and arrested for murder.

The day after his arrest, Joseph Rickards confessed to the crime and his statement duly recorded:

*The voluntary examination and confession of Joseph Rickards, touching the murder of Walter Horseman, &c. taken before me, one of his Majesty's Justices of the peace for the said county, who says, that about August last, he was hired to live with Walter Horseman, a cow keeper, at Kentish Town, and that about a fortnight after he had been in the service, he was sitting one evening with his mistress, Mrs. Horseman, by the kitchen fire, when she pulled his head on her bosom, and seemed very fond of him; that ever since that time she has frequently kissed him, and this informant has laid hold of her breasts, and at several times – but he has never had any other connection of a private nature than what is before mentioned; but she has frequently told him she wished her husband was dead; that on Friday, the 10th of February inst. about six o'clock in the evening he shut the back door that goes into the yard, and went up stairs and hid himself in the closet, described by the several informants in the information, and about two o'clock in the morning he came out of the closet and went into the room where Horseman lay, with the stick he left in the room, and now in possession of John Berringer the headborough, but on seeing an iron bar standing in the chimney corner, he took the bar and wounded the said Walter Horseman, and struck him several blows on the head and fact [face], and then made his escape out of a window in Horseman's room, opened the back gates, and run away over the fields, and returned again in the morning to Kentish Town, the farthings he gave the watchman he took out of a closet in Horseman's room, and that no person whatever knew any thing of the matter but this examinant.*

Young Joseph Rickards' confession and other evidence were considered by the jury at his trial on 22 February 1786 at the Old Bailey Sessions and, as expected, he was found guilty of the wilful murder of Walter Horseman.[11] Following a lengthy denunciation of the 'heinous' crime, Mr Justice Gould passed sentence, and addressing the prisoner proclaimed,

*you [will] be carried from hence to the place from whence you came, and from thence to the place of execution, there to be hanged by the neck till you are dead; and that your body be delivered to be dissected and anatomised, according to the statute, and the Lord have mercy on your sinful soul.*

In epilogue to the evidence, Joseph Rickards recanted some of his earlier accusations levelled at Mary Horseman declaring, 'she is innocent of every thing I have accused her with.' So, what was the motive behind the crime? To this Rickards gave no explanation, except for a simple, 'I don't know.' It is more than likely that, as a result of his infatuation with Mary Horseman, he took her momentary desire to wish her husband dead quite literally and naively obliged. Closing the case, the court announced that the sentence should be carried out as near as conveniently possible to where the murder took place. So it was that, at 7.40 am on 27 February 1786, Joseph Rickards left Newgate Prison to be executed in a field opposite Horseman's dairy in Kentish Town. He requested to see Mary Horseman for one final time. She was sent for but had gone to London. Doubtless disappointed, Joseph left this world with but one journey remaining. This was back to the City and the awaiting dissection slab at Surgeons' Hall.

Some nine months later, what was left of the body of young Joseph was to be joined by three High Holborn malefactors. These also suffered the indignity of being publicly hanged near to where their crime was committed. The trio were indicted for:

> *That they not having the fear of God before their eyes, but being moved and seduced by the instigation of the devil, on the 16th day of November last [1786], with and arms, upon one Duncan Robertson, in the peace of God and our Lord the King then and there being, feloniously, wilfully, and of their malice aforethought, did make an assault, and that he, the said Michael Walker, with a certain knife, made of iron and steel, value 6d. which he in his right hand then and there had and held, upon the left shoulder, forehead, nose and wrist of the said Duncan, did cut, flab, and penetrate, giving him with the knife aforesaid, divers mortal wounds, one on the left shoulder, of the length of six inches, and of the depth of one inch, one other wound on his forehead and nose of the length of two inches, and of the depth of one inch, of which he lingered till the 20th of November, and then died; and that the said Richard Payne and John Cox were present, aiding, assisting and comforting the said Michael Walker, to do and commit the said murder; and so the Jurors say, that they the said Michael Walker, Richard Payne, and John Cox, him the said Duncan Robertson in manner and form aforesaid, did kill and murder.*

Thus opened the proceedings in the trial of Walker, also known as Irish Mich or Myke, and associates at the Old Bailey Sessions on Friday, 15 December 1786.[12] The court heard that, on 16 November at about 5.40 pm, having visited his sister in Lombard Street, Duncan Robertson and friend, Isaac Hunt, were walking along High Holborn near Smart's Buildings, when the latter felt a person steal a book from his pocket. The pocket book was quickly passed to an accomplice but Hunt managed to apprehend his thief, Michael Walker, and coolly proceeded to march him to a nearby magistrate. En route, a scuffle broke out and Hunt's companion was fatally stabbed. It transpired that Walker inflicted the mortal wound, aided and abetted by Richard Payne, with the third member of the villainous gang, fifteen-year-old John (alias Robert) Cox, looking on. Having fled from the scene of the crime, whilst apparently making a 'huzza' (a celebratory noise) and laughing, the trio were later seen drinking in the nearby *Bull* alehouse, Newtoner's Lane (now Macklin Street). Both before and after the event, several shopkeepers along High Holborn recognised the perpetrators and later gave evidence to this fact at the trial. There seems to have been no mistake about the three being in the vicinity of the crime. Despite the efforts of a surgeon, poor Robertson finally succumbed to his wounds on 20 November and now Walker, Payne and Cox were wanted for murder.

Walker was apprehended in the *White Hart* public house, also in Newtoner's Lane, by Officer Jacob Freeman of Hyde Street Police Office. In spite of a knife being found on his person that could well have been the murder weapon, Walker protested his innocence and claimed mistaken identity. He was, nonetheless, taken into custody. The capture of Richard Payne was not so easy. Payne has disappeared from the area completely. Joshua Parish, a vigilant pub landlord, happened to notice a newspaper advertisement requesting anyone with knowledge of the whereabouts of the assailant to come forward. He felt he knew Payne as someone who had recently been enlisted into the East India Company by agents recruiting at his pub. He dutifully informed his local police office, which, in turn, dispatched Officer Freeman and Isaac Hunt to a Company ship moored at Gravesend in order to identify and, if successful, arrest the fugitive. On board the outward bound *Princess Royal*, Hunt recognised Payne – now under the pseudonym of James Davis – in an impromptu line up. On the journey back to London, Payne confessed to his part in the incident but denied murder. Likewise, John Cox admitted his part, namely handling Hunt's pocket book, but denied any other role in the affair.

The case against the three was more than convincing. In his defence, Walker argued that 'he knew nothing about it.' Payne again protested his innocence as to the murder and Cox pleaded that he too was 'innocent as a child unborn.' Their protestations fell on deaf ears and the jury found the trio guilty of wilful murder. Before announcing the inevitable sentence, the court recorder comments upon the prisoners' contemptuous attitude towards the crime, 'Instead of being struck with awe at the crime you had committed, you are found in the most flagitious manner, huzzaing and glorying in your crime.' The aftermath of the trial is perhaps best summoned up in a contemporary newspaper account of their punishment:

*Yesterday morning* [Monday, 18 December 1786] *Michael Walker, alias Irish Myke, Richard Payne, alias James Davis, and Robert Cox, a boy of about fifteen, convicted on Friday last at the Old Bailey, for the wilful murder of Mr Duncan Robertson, near Smart's Buildings, High Holborn, were executed on a gibbet erected near the spot where the horrid fact was committed. They were taken from Newgate in a cart about eight o'clock.*

*Walker and Payne appeared to be almost in a state of stupidity, though the former had a book in his hand, at which he frequently looked, but not as if the contents seemed to have any considerate effect upon him. The cries and lamentations of the boy were incessant, and so loud as to be heard at a great distance: he frequently exclaimed, 'The Lord have mercy on my soul! Christ receive my soul!' The cart drew from under the gallows about nine, and after hanging an hour, the bodies were taken to Surgeons' Hall for dissection.* [13]

These few cases have highlighted the full force of eighteenth-century punitive reprisal for those convicted of wilful murder. They of course represent only a token example of many such murders but whether a crime of passion, an alcohol fuelled assault or the result of a menial theft, all those found guilty received more than just reckoning for their crimes. Nevertheless, as the second part of this chapter looking at eighteenth-century criminal misdemeanour demonstrates, murder was not the only crime for which lawbreakers could swing or suffer dramatic retribution.

**Part two: Misdemeanour – fraud, trespass and juvenile crime**
Forgery and counterfeiting of coins, or coining, was punishable by death. This seemingly harmless crime was considered treason against the Crown and would not be tolerated. But, with motive synonymous with profit, death was no deterrent to those forging in the many back street workshops located in St Pancras and, in particular, Holborn during this period. Often the practice was family-run, with husband and wife teams industriously sharing the workload but, as with all traitorous activities, hanging awaited those exposed.

Middle-aged coiners Edward and Deborah Lloyd were to experience this when their coining operation ended in exposure. On 15 July 1745, the couple were accused and indicted for 'feloniously and traitorously' making and passing,

*twenty-four pieces of false, feigned, and counterfeit money and coin, made of copper, pewter, tin, lead, and other base metals, each of the said pieces to the likeness and similitude of a good, lawful and current piece of silver money and coin of this realm, called a shilling.*

At their trial on 11 September 1745, the prosecution's star witness was Joanna Wood, an accomplice of the Lloyds. [14] Following her arrest after attempting to pass on a 'bad' shilling at the *Lord Cobham's Head* public house, Coldbath Fields, Wood decided to give evidence against the Lloyds, as she was 'tired of that way of life.' She testified that the couple had been coining for over twenty-five years; an accusation strenuously denied by Edward Lloyd. His wife also denied any wrongdoing, '[my] poor hands are not fit for coining.' In a trial verging on comedic, the Lloyds suggested that Wood's confession was motivated by revenge. It appeared that Wood had wanted to wed Lloyd, even though he was already married! Incensed by Wood's lies and betrayal, Edward Lloyd proceeded to cast doubt upon her testament and character:

> *Here is but one single witness against us, (and the laws of England require two) and that is Joanna Wood, and she is no witness at all, for the laws of England say, that no single person shall be an evidence against another, unless their character be as clear as the sun; and she is as dark as ever she can be; she is as spotted as ever she can be; a rainy night cannot be darker. No person, especially one so dark as she, ought to be admitted to take another person's life away. There was nothing found in my room relating to coining.*

The jury on the other hand did find Wood's character to be as 'clear as the sun' and the traitorous duo were sent to the gallows.

A crime carrying a lesser sentence was that of trespass. A number of years before the Lloyd's launched their self-financing business in Holborn, Jasper Arnold and William Goddard were found guilty of an

*St Andrew's Church, Holborn, c.1800.*

unusual case of trespass in the parish church of St Andrew, Holborn in 1717. In order to destroy evidence of a bigamous marriage, Goddard enlisted the help of Arnold to tear two pages from St Andrew's *Register-Book of Marriages*. Apparently, Goddard had married Rachel Small in June 1711 but had later married again whilst still being legally wed to his first wife. St Andrew's eagle-eyed clerk, Mr Hopley, had cause to search the marriage register only to find that the pages covering the entire month of June (1711) were missing. As Hopley's deputy, Arnold had access to the register and therefore was a prime suspect. He was duly questioned and admitted the trespass. Having been found guilty at their trial at the Old Bailey Sessions on 4 December 1717, the two were fined and sentenced to the pillory.[15] To be punished publicly in the pillory was a way of destroying the reputation of the convict, whilst also signalling public distaste for the crime. Those sentenced were placed on a platform with arms and head placed through holes in the wooden pillory structure. Duration in the contraption was normally one hour, during which the crowd often expressed their disapproval of the offence by pelting criminals with anything to hand, such as rotten eggs and vegetables, mud and excrement, and even stones and bricks!

Foul deeds were not just restricted to adult perpetrators. Criminals sometimes learned their trade early, as in the case of ten-year-old Richard Henson. On 8 September 1747, young Richard and fellow accomplice, Edward Wood, removed a freshly washed linen sheet hanging on a hedge adjoining a house in Hampstead. The boys carried it wet to London where they attempted to pawn it. Eventually they exchanged the sheet in a bakers shop for a couple of bread rolls. They were later identified as the culprits but, at their trial, Wood informed the court that Henson actually stole the sheet. Poor Richard was consequently sentenced to a whipping.[16] Similarly, a physical punishment was also exacted on John Adams, a St Pancras youth, in 1732. John was indicted for the murder of Lawrence Howard.[17] With other friends, both boys were playing 'Buff-at-the-Bear', a popular children's game. A quarrel ensued between the two, resulting in Howard challenging Adams to a fight in the long field by St Pancras (Old) Church Burial Ground. As arranged, the boys met the following day and according to later evidence, 'they met, fought fair; but the Prisoner striking the Deceas'd an unlucky Blow on the Head, it broke some of the Blood Vessels, and he dy'd the next Day.' John Adams was found guilty of manslaughter and sent for branding: a letter denoting the type of crime was often branded on a prisoner's thumb.

Whether the physical punishments inflicted on these young offenders were sufficient to deter them from a future life of crime is unknown.

*St Pancras (Old) Church, 1752. The fields surrounding the Church (far right) witnessed many activities during the eighteenth century, including a children's game of 'Buff-at-the-Bear' in 1732 that had fatal consequences.*

Yet, despite the harsh penalties that awaited the guilty, committing a foul deed during the eighteenth century in Hampstead, Holborn and St Pancras appeared to be one way of attempting to solve life's problems and, for those who believed this, motive enough.

# CHAPTER 5

# The Hangman's Hanging Offence
## 1750

*John Thrift, hangman, was convicted and sentenced to swing.*

From 1735 until his death in 1752, John Thrift was London's public hangman except, that is, for a break in service in 1750, when he faced the rope himself!

The executioner's career was one of mixed fortune. On one occasion Thrift hanged a man named Thomas Reynolds at Tyburn. After being pronounced dead, Reynolds was laid to rest in an awaiting coffin but, much to the crowd's amazement and delight, he sat up very much alive. Thrift attempted to hang Reynolds for a second time but was stopped by the indignant crowd, who felt that the prisoner had suffered enough. So they rushed the scaffold, attacked Thrift and carried Reynolds off for treatment. The latter died a little while later, presumably from injuries sustained from his attempted hanging. John Thrift's career also included the beheading of Jacobite sympathiser Lord Lovat in 1748. After the Jacobite rebellion of 1745, it became Thrift's responsibility to behead the rebel aristocracy instead of simply suspending them. Supposedly for his role in the anti-Jacobite reprisals, the executioner became the occasional target of public resentment. It was on 11 March 1750 that one such occasion arose. Thrift was driven to chase and fatally strike an alleged tormentor, David Farris, who died eight days later from his wounds.

Indicted for murder, John Thrift stood trial at the Old Bailey Sessions on 25 April 1750.[18] Heard first was the evidence for the prosecution. This was provided by Rebecca Farris, the victim's wife, and two friends, Patrick Farrell and Timothy Garvey. Their testimonies, as to their encounter with the hangman, were consistent and best summed up by Rebecca Farris:

*My husband, Patrick Farrel[l], Timothy Garv[e]y, and myself, were coming by the Prisoner's Door, on the 11th of March, between five and six in the evening* [Thrift and his wife Mary lived in Coal or Cole Yard (now Stukeley Street) in the parish of St Giles]; *Patrick Farrel[l] said to the deceased, David, Do you know that Man? (meaning the prisoner, who was then standing at his own door). No, says he, I do not, I never saw him in my life to my knowledge. The prisoner's wife sitting at the door overheard the words, and said, you pack of Thieves, suppose it is Jack Ketch, do you want to rob him?* [John Catch (aka Jack Ketch) was the London executioner between 1678 and 1686. Following a particularly bungled beheading, Ketch was removed from office. After this, all London hangmen were popularly known as 'Jack Ketch'.] *Said Patrick Farrel*[1], *I do not want to rob him and if I have given offence, I am sorry for it. Then the prisoner came out of his house, and struck this Farrel in the Face two or three times, with his fist; he was not satisfied with that, but he went back, pulled off his coat, hat, and wig, and was then in a flannel waistcoat without sleeves; he went in and fetch'd a Cutlass, drawed it, delivered the scaboard* [Scabbard] *to his wife, and pursued the three men, who were then got to the head of the Cole yard, Drury-lane.*

*St Giles-in-the-Fields parish map, published in 1720, showing Coal (or The Cole) Yard, home to public executioner John Thrift.*

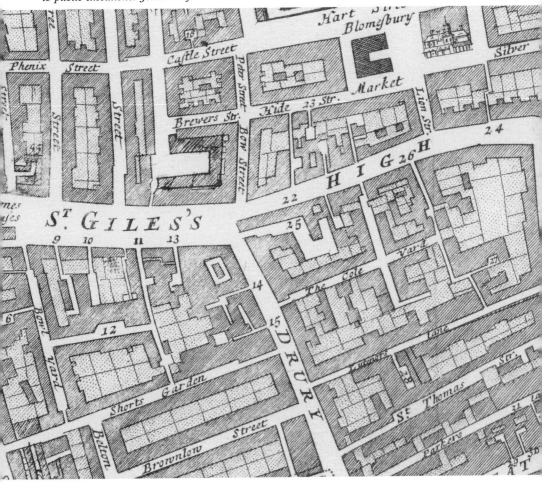

Rebecca Farris's evidence, however, conflicted with testimonies received from a number of independent witnesses. Thomas Clutton and Alice Waring attested:

> *I* [Thomas] *was sitting at the Nine-pin house door, the time these three men, and one woman, was going by the door; I heard this last Witness* [Farrell] *call the prisoner's Wife whore several times, and an eternal whore; after which the prisoner came out of his house, and said, What do you want to rob the house? ... There were four men and two women just pass'd, and in about a quarter of an hour after I* [Alice] *saw a great mob about the prisoner's door. Just as they were gone the prisoner took off his coat, his hat and wig was off before, then he took off his neckcloth, and unbuttoned the neck of his shirt, and followed the men.*

Other accounts reported that an angry mob had chased Thrift to his house and besieged it, shouting Jacobite slogans. No form of Jacobitism was mentioned in evidence but clearly the fracas in Coal Yard had attracted a multitude of concerned onlookers. In his defence, John Thrift offered the following account of events:

> *I had been twice at St. Giles's church that day, and as I was coming home through Drury-lane, Farrel*[l] *began the quarrel. There were four of them, the deceased's wife was one, with a child in her arms. I turned into the Coal-yard where I live. Blood and* [h]*ounds, said Farrel*[l]*, do you know who this is coming along? No, said the deceased, I do not know him; he said again, that is Jack Ketch , he stole a gold watch, and two silver spoons, and has broke out of Newgate. Said I, go along, you black-guard dog; they said, there was ten guineas reward for taking of me. Farrel*[l] *knock'd me down at my own door. I strove to take the stick out of his hand, the others of them gave me another blow, and knock'd me down again. I desired my wife to fetch the hanger* [cutlass]*, and I do declare it never was out of the scabbard, till Enoch Stock took it out.*

Stock was a long time acquaintance of the hangman, who joined the affray after Thrift began chasing the quartet from his house. Part of Thrift's story was substantiated by witness Patience Jones, who testified that she saw three or four men armed with sticks swearing that they would 'knock his brains out' as he left church. All witnesses, though, were in general agreement as to what happened after John Thrift began pursuing his tormentors, namely the attack upon Farris. That is all with the exception of Thrift himself.

*St Giles-in-the-Fields' Church, 1811. Executioner John Thrift twice visited the church on 11 March 1750 before returning home and killing a heckler.*

There seems to be a consensus that Thrift had left Coal Yard with cutlass in hand then, running across Drury Lane, had caught up with his quarries in Short's Gardens. Surrounded by what Alice Waring believed to be at least 'a thousand people about them', a skirmish ensued. Blows were exchanged, resulting in Thrift delivering a fatal strike to the left side of Farris's head. Witness Philip Lisle described the scene:

*I was sitting at my own door at this time, facing the Green Man, I saw the prisoner in a white waistcoat, and a Scymiter in his hand, follow those people into Drury-lane; he overtook them at a Gateway, and there I saw him take three cuts at the man that is dead ... He [Thrift] said, he had been besieged, and he was sorry he had not cut one of their heads off.*

William Carrier, local resident endorses this, 'I saw the prisoner at this time strike the deceased one blow on the left side of the head with a hanger; I was about five yards distance, and live directly opposite him.' Evidence weighed heavy against Thrift, who initially denied attacking Faris. He claimed that it was Stock that had grabbed the weapon from his grasp and then administered the crucial blow, 'Enoch Stock did take the hanger out of my hand, and cut this man the deceased.' Thrift later retracted this claim, which at first was not disputed by Stock. The latter was stunned in the mêlée and could not remember what had happened during the fight.

Establishing the true sequence of events leading up to the clash in Short's Gardens proved too difficult for the judiciary to ascertain, especially given the contrary nature of witness testaments. Equally, Thrift's motive for the attack upon Faris remains speculative. Was Thrift tormented into taking desperate measures after he had attended his daily devotions? By now, he would certainly have been a local celebrity and thus fair game for those who sought pleasure in his persecution. His very position as public executioner would indeed attract enemies of relatives and friends of those he attended at Tyburn. Or, as his wife suggests, were the troublesome quartet out to rob his house? This was unlikely, given the well-populated neighbourhood and the notoriety such a burglary would cause by stealing from such a public figure. Although the reason for the prisoner to chase and attack his antagonists remained unclear, the jury's verdict was very clear – guilty. John Thrift, hangman, was convicted and sentenced to swing. Doubtless, many felt this punishment to be poetic justice but this feeling would have been short-lived. The authorities sought and gained a pardon for their public servant. The exact details about his release are unknown but one theory suggests that the establishment had no intention of seeing Jacobitism endorsed by mob activity. Once again, John Thrift was to swing into action as London's executioner; a role he continued for another two years to include the execution of famous highwayman James Maclane less than six months after his own escape from the drop!

CHAPTER 6

# Demanding Satisfaction: The Duelling Fields of St Pancras
## 1790–1843

*Bizarrely, two workers from a piano manufactory fought over the tuning of a piano!*

During the reigns of George III and George IV, the fields around Chalk Farm and Primrose Hill in the parish of St Pancras were notorious as locations for settling 'affairs of honour', and at times even rivalled the great duelling grounds of Wimbledon Common, Battersea Fields and Putney Heath. In his *History of St Pancras*, Samuel Palmer keenly observed, '[Chalk Farm is] the favourite place for discontented men to meet in order to settle their differences with the pistol, as if gunpowder were the stronger argument, and a steady aim the best logic.'[19] Later, during the early years of Queen Victoria's sovereignty, the outskirts of Camden Town also gained notoriety for playing host to one last 'demand for satisfaction'.

Illegal as the activity was, numerous accounts of duels have been recorded and reasons for pistols at dawn are equally plentiful and

*A panoramic view of Primrose Hill and the Chalk Farm looking north, c.early nineteenth century. During this period the fields surrounding the hill witnessed many 'duels to the death'.*

The Trial of Nerves *by DT Egerton, (date unknown). With the capital providing a picturesque backdrop, the etching depicts the settling of an 'affair of honour' on Primrose Hill.*

outlandish. One of the earliest duels on record to have taken place around Chalk Farm was that between Captain Harvey Aston and Lieutenant Fitzgerald of the 60th Regiment on Friday, 25 June 1790; a lady being the cause of argument. Fitzgerald had the opening discharge and shot Aston through the neck. The latter recovered but was fatally shot in another duel a few years later. On Wednesday, 6 April 1803, Lieutenant-Colonel Robert Montgomery and Captain James MacNamara RN met at Chalk Farm to settle a dispute originating in Hyde Park. The quarrel on this occasion did not concern female honour but related to the duellists' dogs! A dog of one officer snarled at the dog of the other. The duel was fought and what was initially a natural spat between pets became a case of murder. Montgomery was mortally wounded and expired in a room at the *Chalk Farm* tavern. Although seriously injured, MacNamara recovered and was tried for murder at the Old Bailey but, with excellent character references from the Lords Nelson and Hood and many others, he was found not guilty.

Not every demand for satisfaction at Chalk Farm was successfully completed. Three years after Montgomery and MacNamara stood face to face, an encounter between Tom Moore and Francis Jeffrey took place at the location in 1806. Despite having seconds in attendance, as well as being shielded by trees in an attempt to conceal the activity, the duel came to an abrupt end by the arrival of Bow Street runners who emerged from a hedge just before the signal to take aim was given. Suitably disarmed by the runners, the protagonists argued that the pistols were loaded only with blank cartridges. When recollecting the event, Moore believed a friend alerted Bow Street Police Office as to the impending affair of honour. Moore and Jeffrey later became amiable friends.

Not to be outdone by affairs involving women and pets, a case of duelling pianos or rather piano tuners was recorded in 1809. Bizarrely, two workers from a piano manufactory fought over the tuning of piano! A newspaper report dated 3 October proffered the following detail:

> *Tuesday last, an affair of honour took place, near Chalk Farm between two journeymen in the employ of Messrs Broadwood and Co., piano-forte-makers, which originated in a dispute; respecting the tuning of an instrument! At an early hour the parties met, attended by their seconds at the bottom of Primrose Hill, when after exchanging two shots, one of the combatants, either supposing himself wounded, or apprehending the consequences of a third fire, dropped down. Some labourers; whom the report of the pistols had attracted, coining up at the time, and his adversary taking them for Police Officers, immediately made his escape.*[20]

Not all duels held in the vicinity were fought to settle personal arguments. In fact, some involved men who had no individual axes to grind with each other. Such an example is the duel that occurred on 12 January 1818 between former Battle of Waterloo veteran Theodore O'Callaghan and Lieutenant Edmund Bailey of the 58th Regiment.[21] It transpired that the duel was a result of a misunderstanding in the organisation of another duel that never actually took place. O'Callaghan and Bailey were acting as seconds for separate friends in an affair of honour that was to occur the day before. It was understood that the parties would meet to give satisfaction near Chalk Farm either at the *White Hart* or at another public house called the *Load of Hay*. Mr O'Callaghan and party duly arrived at the *White Hart* at the agreed time, whilst Lieutenant Bailey and company made their way to the *Load of Hay.* Needless to say, believing there to be a no-show from the other party, each took their charges away. Looking for an explanation, O'Callaghan and Bailey placarded each other's combatants and charged each other with deliberately avoiding to meet that morning. In the verbal mêlée that ensued, O'Callaghan and Bailey shouldered the blame for the mix up and agreed to duel each other the following morning at a field near the *Load of Hay* pub.

Mr Adams, who occupied a house in Ingram Lane near the pub, witnessed the combat from his upstairs window that overlooked the field of battle. It was about 9 am on Monday morning on the aforementioned date that, whilst dressing, Mr Adams heard the sound of two pistols discharging. He suspected that two gentlemen were duelling and, looking out of his window, saw four men in a field. Dressing quickly, he arrived at the scene to find his suspicions justified. Mr Adams found that, although still on his legs, Lieutenant Bailey had been shot. He noticed that Bailey had sustained a mortal wound to his stomach, near the navel, and that the ball had almost gone right through him. With the help of O'Callaghan and the two seconds, Bailey was transported five hundred yards back to Mr Adam's house, where he was deposited on a sofa.

Soon after, a surgeon was urgently summoned from Hampstead. The medical man removed the ball from Bailey's wound and, still conscious, the dying man requested that full particulars about the affair be conveyed to his father in Limerick. He then summoned O'Callaghan to his death-sofa and asked to shake hands with him in friendship. As they shook, Bailey forgave his killer and told him that everything had been conducted in the most honourable way. A short but rather poignant exchange between the duellists then followed. O'Callaghan forwarded, 'I wish I had been wounded in the room as you; I felt your first ball about my legs, and I only wish it had taken affect.' Bailey replied, 'God bless you, and I thank you for your attention.' Optimistically, O'Callaghan then announced, 'Never mind, my good fellow, in about a fortnight or three weeks time we shall be walking down Bond Street together.' But, the injured man knew otherwise, 'No; I have seen the sun rise this morning but I shall never see it set again.' Then, after forgiving and bidding farewell to both seconds, he died about an hour later. O'Callaghan and the seconds were taken to Bow Street and charged with murder. In law, anyone assisting at a duel in which a participant was killed was also guilty of murder. After being committed to Newgate Prison, their trial took place at the Old Bailey on 14 January 1818. All pleaded not guilty, with the prisoners receiving excellent character testaments from a number of military and other

*A typical trial at the Sessions House, Old Bailey, as depicted in the* Newgate Calendar *published in 1815.*

gentlemen. The jury deliberated for just ten minutes and returned a verdict of manslaughter against all three. Each was sentenced to three months imprisonment.

If this duel didn't catch the local imagination the exploits of the next argument certainly attracted a wider audience through its literary connection. On 16 February 1821, at 9 pm on a moonlit night, a field between the *Chalk Farm* tavern and Primrose Hill became the scene of yet another fatal encounter; this time between John Scott, editor of Baldwin's *London Magazine*, and solicitor Jonathan Christie, a friend of John Lockhart, a contributor to the rival *Blackwood's Magazine*. The dispute developed out of some articles in the *London* that criticised Lockhart over his conduct and management of *Blackwood's*. After a series of attempted explanations and non-apologies, and now acting on behalf of Lockhart, who had left London for Edinburgh, Christie found himself unwittingly agreeing to meet with Scott to settle the matter once and for all.

Scott's first shot missed and Christie, in a final attempt to resolve differences, fired away from his target. As protocol demanded, a second exchange was now required. This time, the solicitor's aim was true.

Mortally wounded in the groin, Scott was conveyed to the *Chalk Farm* and here, later, succumbed to his injuries. In panic, Christie and the two seconds, Messrs Traill and Patmore, fled the country. No more was heard of Christie but Traill and Patmore eventually returned of their own freewill to stand trial for murder at the Old Bailey. Fortunately for these, having been influenced by sympathetic trial judge Lord Chief Justice Abbot, the jury returned a verdict of not guilty. With hindsight, this tragic affair would have been best resolved if the parties involved had restricted themselves to duelling with words and not fire-arms! By the 1820s, society at large began to grow weary of such bouts of misplaced bravado, as did the law whose tolerance of such affairs was growing ever shorter. Chalk Farm tired of its violent association with duelling, especially as the vicinity had now began developing as a residential area. And so, north London duellists were forced to seek another place of meeting.

The last duel in the former parish of St Pancras, and allegedly the last of its type in England, didn't take place in Chalk Farm, as one would expect for posterity, but about a mile to the north-east in grounds

*On 1 July 1843, the last duel in St Pancras was fought in grounds adjacent to the* Brecknock Arms *tavern, Camden Town.*

adjacent to the *Brecknock Arms* tavern near Camden Town. Raising their pistols at dawn, around about 5 am on Saturday, 1 July 1843, were Lieutenant Alexander Thompson Munro, Adjutant of the Royal Horse Guards (Blue), and his brother-in-law David Lynar Fawcett, a Lieutenant-Colonel in the 55th (Westmoreland) Regiment. The cause of the duel was apparently a remark made during tea at Fawcett's house by Munro. Whilst on service in China, Fawcett let Munro look after his affairs at home. On his return, Fawcett accused Munro of making a blunder over dealings with a tenant. Incensed by this accusation, Munro retaliated in a furious rage and was ordered from the house by Fawcett. Munro demanded satisfaction

*'The Last Duellist'. Lieutenant Alexander Munro tak* *from the* Illustrated London News.

and, by the following morning, arrangements had been made. Upon duelling, it was Colonel Fawcett who received the fatal gunshot wound.

In the vicinity had been Police Constable Jones. On hearing the gunshot, he quickly rushed to the scene to find Fawcett bleeding from a wound in the chest. Upon asking the injured man as to what was happening, he was curtly answered, 'What is it to you? It was an accident.' Refused help at the nearby *Brecknock Arms*, Fawcett was conveyed south to the *Camden Arms* in Randolph Street, Camden Town. Despite being attended by eminent surgeons, he died two days later at the public house. Meanwhile, Munro, the seconds (Lieutenants David Grant and William Cuddy) and duel-attending surgeon George Gulliver all fled the scene within moments of the fatal shot being fired. Cuddy and Gulliver were later arrested and charged with murder. The principal killer and Grant both made their escape abroad. To alter his appearance, Grant even went to the trouble to shave off his moustache.

Following this latest duelling outrage, public ill feeling against the activity reached an all time high. This led in 1843 to the founding of the Anti-Duelling Association whose aim was to abolish the practice, describing it as 'sinful, irrational and contrary to the laws of God and man.' Even *The Times* (20 July 1843) championed the cause and, citing the Brecknock duel, commented:

> *If anything were wanting to strip the horrible practice of duelling of that unhappy idea of chivalry and honour with which in most minds it is blindly associated, it must be found in the circumstances of the late duel between Colonel Fawcett and Lieutenant Munro.*

Meanwhile, on 25 August 1843, the murder trial of Cuddy and Gulliver took place at the Central Criminal Court, Old Bailey. Owing to being present at the duel to potentially save life, the case against Gulliver was dropped and Cuddy too was found not guilty. Grant surrendered himself in December and stood trial in 1844. He was also acquitted. Lieutenant Alexander Munro, on the other hand, remained on the continent. Stripped of his commission, he was finally tried in August 1847 and was found guilty. Despite his disappearance overseas, leniency was shown and Munro was sentenced to one year's imprisonment in Newgate. The final twist in this infamous case befell the widow of Colonel Fawcett. Although Mrs Fawcett re-married, she was refused an army pension normally awarded to widows of high-ranking officers. This was to be a sad epitaph to a foul and illegal incident that has since become notorious as the last 'demand for satisfaction' to have taken place in the former duelling fields of St Pancras.

# CHAPTER 7

# A Poisonous Verdict: The Wrongful Execution of Eliza Fenning
## 1815

*It was reported that she was carried from the dock 'convulsed with agony and uttering frightful screams.'*

The most tragic story of all the cases featured in this book concerns that of twenty-one-year-old Eliza Fenning. Wrongly accused of poisoning her employer and his family, Eliza was tried, convicted and hanged for attempted murder. To this day, the identity of the real perpetrator of the crime has never been confirmed but he or she lived with the knowledge that an innocent young lady swung in their place.

Early in 1815, Eliza Fenning had secured the position of cook to the household of Mr Robert Gregson Turner and his wife, Charlotte. The couple resided at 68 Chancery Lane, Holborn, where, in addition to Eliza, a housemaid and two apprentices, one named Roger Gadsden, were also employed. In 2005, a number of small businesses, near the junction with High Holborn occupy the site. On Tuesday, 21 March 1815, Eliza was informed that Robert Turner's father, Orlibar Turner, would be joining his son for dinner that afternoon. The meal included beefsteak and yeast dumplings, which Eliza had dutifully prepared earlier in the day. Sitting down to dinner, the food was heartily consumed; even Eliza and young Gadsden had eaten some of the main course an hour or so before her master and family commenced to dine.

All was well during the meal but, shortly after, the Turners began to complain of severe stomach pains and nausea. Eliza and Roger also began to feel unwell. Dr John Marshall was summoned to attend the sickly household. He nursed those stricken down through the night and was pleased when, the following morning, all ailments began to subside and full recovery appeared to be underway. Nursing duties over, Marshall began to suspect foul play was involved; never mind that food poisoning was then quite common and often due to inadequate culinary and personal hygiene. The doctor's suspicions were partly justified when, upon thoroughly examining the contents of the mixing dish in which the dumplings had been prepared, he found traces of arsenic. The poison was to be found in many homes for use in the battle against vermin, and 68 Chancery Lane proved to be no exception.

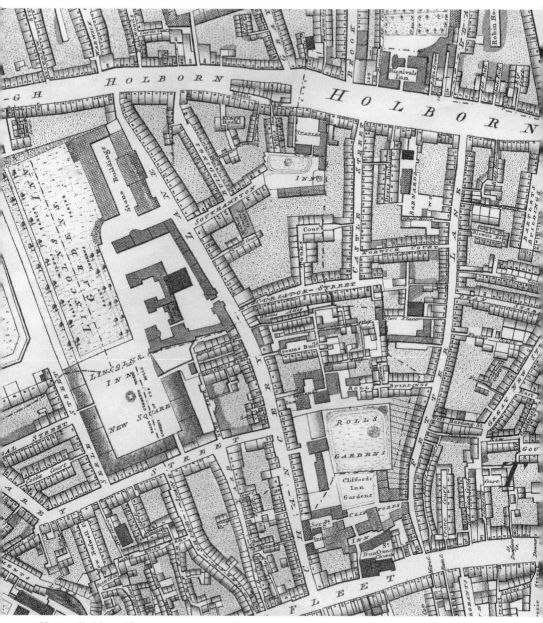

*Horwood's Map of London 1792–98. The Turner's house at 68 Chancery Lane was located on the east side of the street near the junction with High Holborn.*

Indeed, a small parcel containing the substance was kept in the kitchen drawer and clearly marked 'Arsenic, poison' in large characters. Notwithstanding that anyone had access to the drawer, the kitchen and its contents were perceived to be Eliza's domain and hence her responsibility. Therefore, as she was the only one to have prepared the dumplings, suspicion immediately fell upon her.

In a published account of the matter, Dr Marshall recorded:

> *Eliza Fenning cleared the table of the remains of the dumplings. Mrs. R. Turner observed to her that 'the dumplings were by no means what she expected.' The cook made no reply, but blushed, and appeared in great agitation, of the cause of which her mistress was then unconscious, as at that time the poison had not begun to operate … The cook had dined with the other servants at two o'clock, and not till after she had heard of the distressing scene that was passing up stairs, and had cautioned Mr. Gadsden not to touch the dumplings, did she eat of them. This deliberation carries the strongest proof of her conviction; as knowing she was the cause of mischief, she was determined to destroy herself to evade justice.*[22]

Upon Eliza finding out that the matter was to be officially investigated, the doctor further reported that, 'she became giddy, and fell down, when sufficiently recovered, she put on her clothes, and shewed a strong disposition to escape out of the house; to prevent which the outer and inner doors were secured.' The evidence-shy conclusions of Marshall were seemingly enough to convince the Turners and the authorities that Eliza was guilty of the foul deed. She was duly arrested and charged with attempted murder.

Eliza strenuously denied adding the poison to the dumpling dough. She suggested that the milk used in the accompanying sauce made by housemaid Sarah Peer was perhaps to blame but this theory was flawed; two of those struck down had not partaken of the sauce. Additionally, Mrs Turner described the dumplings themselves as being dark, leaden and flat and 'by no means what she expected.' This suggested that the dough mix had been corrupted and that it must have been done so by the cook's own hand, as she alone was solely responsible for dinner preparations. Theories soon abounded regarding Eliza's motive for committing the deed. Apparently, Caroline Turner had earlier caught a scantily clad Eliza cavorting with Roger Gadsden and assumed that she was in the process of seducing the young apprentice. Finding the scene abhorrent to her sensibilities, Mrs Turner threatened Eliza with dismissal. The cook's supposed bawdy behaviour was unlikely, especially as she was due to be married later that year; the date planned for nuptials was to prove cruelly portentous. Therefore, having been allegedly discovered with Gadsden, the household believed that Eliza used the arsenic in revenge against her mistress; the fact that she decided to exact retribution on all, including herself, seemed foolhardy in the least. Another incidental example indicating her supposed guilt was forwarded by Dr Marshall:

> *Her* [Eliza's] *vindictive spirit, and want of veracity, were additionally displayed by a desire to criminate several members of Mr Turner's family: a fortnight after imprisonment, she daily endeavoured to implicate her fellow servant, Sarah Peer; then removed the charge.*

These assertions, coupled with the allegation of inappropriate behaviour, with vengeance as motive, seemed to have confirmed what many had believed – guilty as charged. This so-called evidence was, of course, purely circumstantial but it was enough to place Eliza in the dock.

Following an appearance before the magistrate, Eliza Fenning was remanded in custody at Newgate Prison prior to her trial next door at the Sessions House, Old Bailey. This was set to commence on Wednesday, 5 April. Facing her peers, the cook was indicted thus:

*The Sessions House, Old Bailey, as featured in the* Newgate Calendar *published in 1815. Conveniently, Newgate Prison was also located in Old Bailey adjacent to the Sessions House.*

*That she, on the 21st day of March 1815, feloniously and unlawfully did administer to, and cause to be administered to, [Orlibar] Turner, Robert Haldebart Gregson Turner and Charlotte Turner, his wife, certain deadly poison to wit, arsenic, with intent the said persons to kill and murder.*

The prosecution examined the events before and after the fateful meal, with Orlibar, Robert and Charlotte Turner, Roger Gadsden and Dr Marshall amongst the witnesses. After attending to his patients' complaints, which he suspected had been caused by arsenic poisoning, the doctor then explained how he discovered the poison in the mixing dish:

*I examined it* [the dish]. *I washed it with a tea-kettle of warm water. I first stirred it and let it subside. I decanted it off. I found half-a-teaspoon of white powder. I washed it a second time. I found it to be decidedly arsenic.*

As to motive, Mrs Turner told the court about discovering the cook in a compromising situation with the apprentice. Having then threatened Eliza with dismissal, she believed that this was motive enough for her cook to seek revenge upon her and the household. In her defence, Eliza called four witnesses, each of whom gave her excellent character references. Alas, as they could not offer any relevant evidence, their statements were considered inconsequential. Ultimately, all Eliza could do was to continue to protest her innocence. That the victims succumbed to deliberately administered arsenic was not under question but could it be proved beyond doubt that Eliza was the culprit? No, but it mattered little. In accepting the biased testaments of the prosecution witnesses, as well as the hearsay and circumstantial nature of the evidence, the trial recorder effectively guided the jury to find the defendant guilty. After a few minutes deliberation, they agreed. Eliza was to hear her fate the following day.

After the trial, Eliza wrote a letter to her fiancé from Newgate Prison in which she lamented, 'They have, which is the most cruellest thing in this world, bought me in guilty ... I may be confined most likely six weeks at least.' Little did she know that the judiciary had other ideas. Returning to receive her 'in-just' reward, Eliza was sentenced to be hanged by the neck until she was dead; the punishment to be carried out on 26 July 1815, the very date that had previously been set for her wedding day! Attempted murder still carried the death penalty, only in 1861 did it cease to be a capital offence. Upon hearing the punishment, Eliza was inconsolable. It was reported that she was carried from the dock 'convulsed with agony and uttering frightful screams.' Believing that a gross miscarriage of justice had occurred, the verdict was very unpopular with the public but, despite appeals for clemency made to the office of the Home Secretary and to the Lord Chancellor, the sentence stood.

Joining Miss Fenning to be hanged outside the Debtor's Door of Newgate Prison were Abraham Adams, convicted of forgery, and William Oldfield, under sentence for rape. At 8.00 am on the day of her execution, Eliza left the condemned cell for the last time to make the short journey to the gallows. Dressed in a fashionable white muslin gown and cap and wearing high laced lilac boots, purported to be her wedding outfit, but with her hands pinioned, she was accompanied in prayer by the Reverend Horace Cotton. To him, she continued to protest her innocence, 'Before the just and almighty God, and by faith of the Holy Sacrament I have taken, I am innocent of the offence with which I am charged.' The noose having been placed around her neck by hangman John Langley, with her arms bound behind and face

covered, all was set for her hanging. At 8.30 am, Langley withdrew the pin releasing the trapdoor. It is said that Eliza fell the carefully calculated drop quietly and easily to her death 'almost without writhing'. As was then custom, her father paid the executioner the fee of fourteen shillings and sixpence before he could take charge of his daughter's dead body for burial.

Poor Eliza's funeral took place five days later on 31 July 1815. At 3.30 pm, a vast procession of mourners left the Fenning's family home in Eagle Street, near Red Lion Square, and headed north

*The condemned cell at Newgate Prison where many convicted murderers spent their final days prior to their execution.*

towards St George the Martyr Burial Ground (now St George's Gardens) via Lamb's Conduit Street and the Foundling Hospital. *The Times* (1 August 1815) detailed the scene:

> *It* [the procession] *was preceded by about a dozen peace officers, and these were followed by nearly 30 more; next came the undertaker, immediately followed by the body of the deceased. The pall was supported by six young females, attired in white: then followed eight persons, male and female, as chief mourners, led by the parents. These were succeeded by several hundreds of persons, two and two, and the whole was closed by a posse of peace officers. Many thousands accompanied the procession, and the windows, and even tops of the houses, as it passed, were thronged with spectators.*

The report goes on to mention that the event was conducted in a peaceful manner, except that is for a young man, a livery servant, in the crowd who 'had spoken somewhat disrespectfully of the deceased, [and, as a result] was rather roughly handled by the populace.' During Eliza's interment, reputedly witnessed by a crowd of nearly 10,000 sympathisers, her mother succumbed emotionally and fainted several times, such was her grief at the sad loss of her daughter.

Meanwhile, the multitude had not forgotten the prosecutors in this sad case. Later that evening, the Turners were troubled by 'a crowd of persons of the lowest order' who had congregated outside their Chancery Lane residence. Constables were called in to disperse the mob, which finally evaporated during the early hours of the next day. Much doubt continued to remain over Eliza's guilt but, if innocent as most believed, who was the culprit and what was his or her motive? Was it a harmless prank perpetrated by one of the household staff that backfired or was it something more calculated? One theory suggests that the real poisoner was a nephew of Orlibar Turner who, at the time, was in conflict with his uncle over an unpaid allowance. It was rumoured but never substantiated that, whilst on his deathbed, the aggrieved relative confessed to stealing into an empty kitchen and sprinkling a quantity of arsenic into the dumpling mixture. As for Eliza, denied a happy marriage and prosperous life, she will be forever known as the unfortunate cook who was victim to a very poisonous verdict.

# CHAPTER 8

# In the Line of Duty: The First Metropolitan Police Deaths 1830–33

*... even the beaten wife joined in the attack against the young officer.*

I n 1829, under the new *Metropolitan Police Act* instigated by Robert Peel, a centralised police force of some 3,000 men was set up and, except for the City of London, became responsible for policing the entire Metropolitan area. Formerly, detection and apprehension of felons in the capital relied upon a somewhat haphazard structure of law enforcement, involving constables, justice of the peace officers, night watches and, during the eighteenth century, the notorious thief-takers. Bow Street runners, under the orders of magistrates, were later employed to apprehend criminals and even private citizens played a major role in identifying and arresting culprits.

It was anticipated that the new 'Bobbies' or 'Peelers' (named after Peel), resplendent in new uniform and armed with truncheons, would patrol the streets in greater numbers in an attempt to prevent crime and deter potential felons. The public did not generally like the new force and it took a few years before these agents of the state gained the trust of those they swore to serve and protect. This aversion may have originated from the fact that many of the initial recruits were of dubious quality and were often drunks and bullies: the first policeman, Constable No.1, was dismissed after only four hours for being drunk on duty! Sadly, it was not long before the first Metropolitan Police officer was murdered in the line of duty.

An early recruit was Constable No. 169 (warrant No. 3170) of S Division, Joseph Grantham. The, doubtless eager, Grantham joined the force on 10 February 1830. On 29 June, his patrol took him into Smith's Place in the then notorious area of Somers Town, a locale still in existence today between Euston and St Pancras Railway Stations. The policeman chanced upon two drunken Irishmen, one named Michael Duggan (a bricklayer), arguing with each other after one of the men had just attacked the other's wife. When attempting to stop the quarrelsome duo from causing a disturbance, Constable Grantham was set upon by the two men. He was knocked to the ground and kicked, even the beaten wife joined in the attack against the young officer. Duggan administered a fatal kick to Grantham's temple and minutes later he lay dead.

At the coroner's inquest, the jury concluded that death was caused 'by the extravasation of some fluid on the brain occasioned by over-exertion in the discharge of his duty.' Charges against Michael Duggan were dropped and he was free to leave the court. As a poignant side story to the incident, Joseph Grantham's wife gave birth to twins the day before his death. Unfortunately, Police Constable Grantham was to be joined in death only six weeks later by his colleague, John Long. This occurred a mere half a mile or so to the south of where Grantham fell protecting the public. For many years Constable Long was believed to be the first Metropolitan Police officer to die in the line of duty but evidence uncovered in 1991 showed that Joseph Grantham was in fact the holder of that distinctly sad honour.[23] Historian John Price noted that, when reporting to the Police Select Committee in 1833, Sir Charles Rowan forgot to mention the earlier casualty and stated that Long had been the first to fall.

Around midnight on Monday, 16 August 1830, Constable No. 43 of G Division, John Long, was patrolling his beat along a stretch of Gray's Inn Road, midway between Battle Bridge (now King's Cross) and High Holborn, when he saw three men behaving suspiciously. Suspecting them of intent to burgle, Long followed the trio, catching up with them close to the gates of St Andrew's Burial Ground (now St Andrew's Gardens), Gray's Inn Road. Moments later a murderous cry was heard by many in the vicinity. *The Times* (19 August 1830) describes how Mary Anne Stevens, a widow and resident of 1 Gray's Inn Road, witnessed the scene:

> *I observed three men coming from the direction of Gray's Inn Lane towards Battle-bridge, and I saw the deceased walking a little way behind them. On a sudden, one of the three men, who wore a blue coat, ran away, and I thought he appeared rather intoxicated. He reeled towards where I stood, and I had full view of his face. He had full dark whiskers, was not young, was full in the face, and rather inclined to corpulency. He also had a scar on the left cheek. At the moment the man ran away, I heard the policeman call out, O God! I am murdered, stop him.*

Widow Stevens further added that she saw the murderer, later identified as John Smith (aka William Sapwell, a baker), raise his arm and strike Police Constable Long. Her story was corroborated by John Cole, a bricklayer of Cromer Street, and Amos Dennis, a local milkman's son. The latter confirmed that Smith alone gave him 'a blow'. It transpired that the policeman had been stabbed in the chest. Within minutes of the incident occurring, fellow officers had arrived on the scene where they

*This drawing by 'Phiz' shows the fatal stabbing of Police Constable Long by John Smith in front of the entrance to St Andrew's Burial Ground, Gray's Inn Road, in 1830.*

found an assortment of housebreaking implements scattered close by. John Long was taken across the street to the home of local surgeon James Holmes at 111 Guilford Street but the medical man found the victim to be dead on arrival. The murder weapon, a shoemaker's knife, was so firmly embedded in Long's chest that the hilt broke off when an attempt was made to remove it. Holmes determined that 'the knife had penetrated the right ventricle of the heart, between the fourth and fifth ribs, and must have unquestionably caused instantaneous death.' Smith was apprehended and taken into custody but, as there was no evidence adduced against them, his cohorts in crime, Henry Summers and Charles Baldwin, were released without charge.

The coroner's inquest took place two days later at the *Crown* tavern, Clerkenwell Green, on 18 August 1830. After the crime, the body had been removed to the vaults underneath St John's Church in Clerkenwell. Unusually, the inquest was heard in the neighbouring parish of St John Clerkenwell. It was normal practice for inquests, and expenses incurred, to be the responsibility of the parish in which death occurred, in this case St Pancras. But on this occasion, owing to the body being moved across the parish boundary, the vestry of St John Clerkenwell was liable for costs. This infuriated St John's vestrymen, whose spokesperson complained that a great irregularity had taken place and requested that the administration be relieved of any expense. Coroner Thomas Stirling firmly rebuked the parish representative's appeal, replying, 'that in a matter of so much importance it did not much signify in what parish the inquiry was held, and as to the expense, it could not be much, and was [therefore] unworthy of consideration.' This was of course no consolation to Constable Long's widow and five children. Despite denying the charge, the be-whiskered and scar faced John Smith was readily identified by several witnesses as the perpetrator of this heinous crime and, as a result, was indicted for murder. He was subsequently found guilty and hanged on 20 September 1830. Smith's remains were then given to St George's Hospital for dissection. Meanwhile, community sympathy for the dead policeman's family was such that 'a liberal public subscription was raised' for its future welfare.

Echoing a similar sentiment was a letter to the editor of *The Times*, dated 22 May 1833. This time, the recipient of sympathy was the wife of Police Constable Robert Culley, whose untimely death occurred whilst on duty during the Coldbath Fields Riot of 1833:

*Sir, I beg to enclose one sovereign for the widow of Robert Culley, the policeman, who lately came to such an untimely end through the violence of the mob at Spa-fields. I am, Sir, your very obedient servant. A FRIEND TO THE NEW POLICE.*

Robert Culley, Constable No. 95 of C Division, was one of the earliest bobbies to have been recruited into the new police. Joining the force on 21 September 1829, he resided in Litchfield Street, Seven Dials, in the parish of St Giles. Like Constable Long, he too was to take his final few breaths whilst staggering wounded along Gray's Inn Road.

On 13 May 1833, twenty-seven-year-old Culley and fellow officers were despatched to prevent the militant National Union of the Working Classes from holding a public rally at Coldbath Fields, which lay to the east of Gray's Inn Road. Organised by a few obscure agitators, a proclamation issued by the Secretary of State had declared the meeting to be illegal. Yet, by early afternoon, a huge crowd had gathered at the site. To counter this, over 500 police officers were assembled in nearby streets, ready to swing into action to disperse the crowds. The opposing

*A dramatic 1950s tabloid re-creation of the Coldbath Fields Riot of 13 May 1833.*

*The* Calthorpe Arms *public house, Gray's Inn Road, 2004. Here, in 1833, Constable Robert Culley died in the arms of a barmaid after being wounded in the Coldbath Fields Riot. The notorious inquest into his death also took place at the pub two days later.*

sides duly met, with the police intent on apprehending the chairman of the Union. During the clash, Constable Culley was separated from his fellow officers and disappeared into a mob that busied itself throwing rocks. Reappearing within moments, but this time clutching his chest, he turned to Constable Thomas Flack and uttered, 'Oh, Tom, I am stabbed, I am done.' Another officer, Samuel Acourt, advised Culley, 'I hope it's not serious, Bob. Try to keep up with the division if you can.' By now bleeding badly, the wounded policeman made his way along Calthorpe Street and into Gray's Inn Road. Reaching the *Calthorpe*

*Arms* public house, Culley collapsed into the arms of its barmaid and, although comforting him in his last minutes, he died. Two other policemen were also stabbed in the affray but these survived their injuries.

The inquest into his death opened on 15 May at the location of his death, the *Calthorpe Arms*. Made up of local propertied tradesmen, the jury were openly hostile to the police whose conduct they believed had been 'ferocious, brutal and unprovoked by the people'. Furthermore, the jury claimed that police intervention at the meeting had been illegal because the Riot Act had not been read to the masses prior to engagement. They even criticised the Government by declaring that it did not take 'proper precautions to prevent the meeting assembling.' The inquest lasted several days and finally, against the wishes of the coroner, again Thomas Stirling, the men of the jury insisted that a verdict of 'justifiable homicide' be recorded. *The Times* (21 May 1833) lambasted the jury's finding and questioned its legal knowledge, 'their [the jury's] observations on the Riot Act demonstrate their ignorance of the law relating to illegal assemblies.' Later, the Court of King's Bench overturned this verdict but a replacement verdict finding Police Constable Culley died as a result of wilful murder was not returned. The matter was left in the hands of the Parliamentary Select Committee investigating the riot. Although a number of protagonists were arrested and charged with offences in connection with the disturbance, the murderer was still at large and a £100 reward was offered for information leading to the arrest and conviction of the guilty party.

The seventeen-strong jury, led by Samuel Stockton, a baker of Cromer Street, became instant celebrities. As a result of their misguided sense of duty, jury members were wined and dined and even presented with commemorative medals, goblets and ceremonial banners by well wishers; a large section of the public were positively dismayed at witnessing police 'march into battle' in rank and file for the first time. Moral sight was lost, however, on Robert Culley, the poor individual who, whilst simply carrying out orders, lost his life in this unfortunate incident. His funeral took place on 17 May at St Anne's Church, Soho, but even this solemn occasion was marred a jeering mob. His pregnant wife, Lucy, was awarded £200 compensation by the Government and press sympathy was to influence public opinion in favour of individual officers. Meanwhile, in joining Constables Grantham and Long, Robert Culley gained immortality in being amongst the first of many brave Metropolitan Police officers to die 'in the line of duty'.

# CHAPTER 9

# Murder in Belsize Park: The Jealous Killing of James De La Rue
## 1845

*Alone with the corpse, the young policemen then experienced a bizarre encounter with a cloaked man walking towards him.*

*The prisoner is in his 20th year, but looks two or three years older. He is about the middle height, and has the appearance of a strong, hardy young man. The expression of his countenance is the reverse of pleasing. There is a settled sullenness and fixedness of purpose in his general aspect, much too marked for any one to fail being struck with it. His features are remarkably large and striking. His eyes are deeply embedded in his face, and his nose and mouth are of unusually large dimensions. He has a narrow retiring forehead, a long face, and flat cheeks. His head is remarkably thin towards the back part, and is surmounted by an ample crop of long dark brown hair, which looks as if never disturbed by comb or brush. The conformation of the head altogether would form a fine study for phrenologists. The existence of the animal propensities is strongly indicated.*

Thus printed the *Pictorial Times* (12 April 1845) in an attempt to describe the criminal physiognomy of Thomas Henry Hocker, sentenced to death for the murder and robbery of James De La Rue in Belsize Park, Hampstead. Hocker's 'animal propensity' had, in fact, already viciously manifested itself upon his friend during the evening of 21 February earlier the same year.

It was baker Edward Hilton who first heard the woeful cries of 'murder!' on the day in question. At around 7 pm, in the dark of a winter's evening, Mr Hilton's working day was coming to a close. He had one last delivery to make to a customer at 10 Haverstock Terrace, Belsize Park, and then he could make his way home to West End, Hampstead. Alarmed at such a cry, the baker alerted Police Constable John Baldock on duty in nearby Hampstead Road (now Haverstock Hill) who, with Sergeant Thomas Fletcher, commenced to investigate the commotion. Their search led them to a field adjacent to Haverstock Terrace. Today, the location is covered by the road junction where Belsize Gardens, Eton Avenue and Primrose Hill Road converge. Shortly, the two policemen came across the bloodied body of a man in his early thirties who, on brief examination, had been battered about

*Thomas Henry Hocker, as portrayed in the* Pictorial Times, *29 March 1845.*

the head with a blunt instrument; a bloodstained stick was found close by. Dutifully, Baldock remained with the victim whilst Fletcher left to seek additional assistance.

Alone with the corpse, the young policemen then experienced a bizarre encounter with a cloaked man walking towards him; the traveller was later identified as being Thomas Hocker. The stranger enquired, 'Hilloa, policeman, what have you got there?' Baldock was further asked if he would like any brandy. This he refused but was persuaded to take a shilling for a drink later. At this point another approached the scene, William Satterthwaite, a shoemaker of Hampstead. He engaged in a brief conversation with the stranger who was now looking for signs of life in the deceased. The cobbler asked, 'Is the man quite dead?' to which the stranger replied, 'Yes, he is quite dead; I have felt his pulse, and it has stopped beating.' The stranger then departed to continue his journey in the direction of the nearby *Swiss Cottage* tavern, leaving Constable Baldock in the company of the shoemaker and the deceased. A little later, Sergeant Fletcher and some other officers arrived and removed the body to Hampstead Police Station, where surgeon Dr Perry was summoned to undertake an examination. The doctor's assessment of the dead man's injuries was brief:

> *Death is attributed to concussion of the brain, the consequence of the external violence. I should imagine the wounds were inflicted by a heavy instrument, such as a stick … appearances lead me to conclude that there must have been many blows.*

The obligatory coroner's inquest was held at Hampstead's *Yorkshire Grey* public house, by which time the victim had been identified as James De La Rue, a thirty-three-year-old music teacher of 55 Whittlebury Street, Euston. A vital piece of evidence in the form of a letter, found in the great-coat pocket of the deceased, had also come to light. Addressed to De La Rue, and requesting a meeting at the usual place, the correspondence appeared to be written by a close lady friend named 'Caroline', who supposedly resided in Adelaide Road, Hampstead. This appeared to be the bait used to lure the unsuspecting tutor to the desolate spot in Belsize Park. The letter alluded to Caroline being with child and begs him to honour her in her predicament, 'You can render me forever light-hearted and happy, or forever heart-broken and conscience stricken. Oh, that a bended knee might procure me the former lot!' Given the nature of De La Rue's wounds, the coroner's jury returned a verdict of wilful murder. During the course of the inquest, the hunt for the killer(s) was already underway and within an extremely short time a suspect was found. A search of the victim's rooms revealed clues suggesting that he enjoyed a friendship with Thomas Henry Hocker, who lived with his brother, James, only a mile or so away at 11 Victoria Terrace (now Barrow Hill Road), St John's Wood. With no time to lose, the police called upon the Hockers and found both at

*The scene of James De La Rue's murder. Shortly after the event, souvenir hunters arrived at the location to collect mementoes of the grisly crime. It was reported that the sightseers were not just confined to 'persons of the lower classes of society'.*

home. Here, they discovered items of blood and mud stained clothing, later identified by their father as belonging to Thomas. The Hocker brothers were duly arrested for the murder and taken into custody to await formal charges. A decision was made to release James Hocker but overwhelming evidence against Thomas dictated that he attend Marylebone Police Court to answer the charge of murder.

Public interest in the case became insatiable. So much so that not only did onlookers flock to both coroner's inquest and magistrate's hearing but they also made regular excursions to the scene of the crime to gather mementos. A contemporary newspaper recorded this gruesome activity:

*The curiosity of the public to witness the scene of the recent murder in the field near Haverstock Terrace, Hampstead, seems to increase day by day. The numbers who visited the spot on Tuesday were greater than on any other preceding day, and they were not confined to persons of the lower classes of society. Several carriages, containing ladies, drove up to the field, and gentlemen on horseback, attended by their grooms, rode across to view the place. Not content with seeing, many brought away boughs and twigs from surrounding trees, and chips from the fence against which the unfortunate man fell after he was struck, and whereon the marks of the bloody fingers of the murderer were imprinted.*[24]

Doubtless many of these macabre souvenir hunters also turned out for James De La Rue's funeral. The route of mourning included Hampstead Road that, on the day, was described as being 'one continued moving mass of human beings'. Burial took place on Friday, 28 February in the graveyard attached to the parish church of St John, Hampstead. Conducted by the Vicar of Hampstead, Reverend Thomas Ainger, the service witnessed no unruly scenes. This was perhaps due to extra police reinforcements drafted in for the occasion. After interment, the day's focus fell upon the *Yorkshire Grey* public house where, 'once opened, it became utterly impossible to close it, in consequence of the crowd that kept flocking in. The large space in front also presented the appearance of a fair.'

Morbid festivities over, the public turned its attention to Thomas Hocker. Evidence was heard in front of magistrate Mr Rawlinson who, after due consideration, had no alternative but to commit Hocker to Newgate Prison to later stand trial for murder. This was arranged for 11 April 1845 at the Old Bailey and, at its commencement, the following indictment (which carried three counts) was read to the court:

*For that he did, on 21st February now past, in the parish of Hampstead, with a stick of the value of one penny, feloniously and wilfully strike one James De La Rue, and inflict upon his head divers mortal wounds, bruises, and lacerations, thereby causing a concussion of the brain, of which said wounds, &c., the said James De La Rue did then and there die and that he, the said Thomas Henry Hocker, did feloniously, wilfully, and with malice aforethought, kill and murder him in manner aforesaid. The second count alleged, that the prisoner, on the same day, did, with a certain blunt instrument, to the jury unknown, and, at the same place, maim, and assault the said James De La Rue, and afterwards with great violence to the ground, kicked him on several parts of his body, inflicting divers and several wounds upon the said body, of which the said James De La Rue did then and there die.*

The third count charged the prisoner with felonious stealing on the same day, and at the same place, and from the 'said James De La Rue, a silver watch of the value of 6*l.*, a chain of the value 1*l.* a ring of the

# TRIAL and Sentence

## OF

# Thos. Hocker

## FOR THE

# Murder OF De la Rue

## AT HAMPSTEAD.

As early as eight o'clock this morning, a great number of gentlemen appeared at the doors of the Old Court to gain admission, to hear this important trial; at ten o'clock the court was crowded to excess.

The Judges having arrived, the prisoner Thomas Hocker was arraigned at the bar, charged with the wilful murder of James De la Rue, at Hampstead. On being asked whether he pleaded guilty or not guilty, he answered not guilty.

The Solicitor General opened the case with a most able address to the jury.

Mr. Clarkson with Mr. Ballantine defended the prisoner.

The witnesses underwent a severe cross-examination. the particulars of which have been already laid before the public

By the side of the deceased's body was found his hat and walking-stick.

A man of the name of Thomas Hocker, a teacher of music, in Victoria Terrace, Saint John's Wood, has been apprehended, through the information of Mr. Watson, landlord of the house where his parents reside, on account of seeing the prisoner with a great sum of money new clothes and other circumstances. After his first examination at Mary-le-bone Police court, two of the detective force proceeded to the father's house, Charles Street, Portland Town, and on searching a upper room, found concealed a pair of the prisoner's trowsers and stockings, covered with blood; they then went to the New Prison, and on examining the cuff of his coat, found that also very bloody. A button was found in the field, which corres-ponds with those worn on his coat. They also found a pair of shoemaker's pincers stained with blood. He has on several occasions used great violence towards his father. The prison-er states that he had the money lent him by a female, but which has been disproved.

During yesterday, the cesspool at the house of the accused's father, as also at his lodging were searched, to see if any thing might be secreted there. The poor father of the alleged murderer offered every facility to the police, and in assisting them in their search he him-self discovered amongst some rubbish a dia-mond ring, of which he at once gave infor-mation. It has been shown to the deceased's brother, who identified it. On further search they discovered the gold chain, which has also been identified to belong to the deceased, and here and there spots of blood, clearly indica-ting that it was taking from the body after the murder was perpetrated.

The above letter appears to be written by the prisoner, as it corresponds with his hand writing. A kid glove has been found belong-ing to the deceased· The prisoners brother is still in custody.

The funeral of the deceased took place yester-day, in the presence of some hundreds of per-sons, at Hampstead New Church·

Important Disclosures—Early this morn-ing a great number of persons assembled round the Yorkshire Grey public house, to get a glimpse of the prisoner, who was brought into the inquest room before Mr. Wakley, by the Deputy governor. THIS DAYS TRIAL, Evi-dence of a painful nature will be adduced, and no doubt a verdict of wilful murder will be returned against the prisoner.

There has scarcely ever been known so many persons to have assembled en such an occassion os this for a number of years. the crowds of persons were still greater than on the occassion of Greenacre Cor-voisier, or any murderer that has been -ried in this court. The conversation be-tween the persons outside, was whether the prisoner would be found guilty, some saying they all ought to be hung together.

Smith, Printer, Tottenham Court Road.

*The public's desire for information about Hocker's trial was insatiable, as this account published contemporaneously demonstrates.*

value of 2*l*., and twelve sovereigns, with other monies, from his person.'
To all charges he pleaded 'Not guilty', in a firm voice.

Defending a neatly dressed Hocker were Messrs Clarkson and
Ballantine. However, believing his legal skills to be greater, the
prisoner dismissed his barristers in order to defend himself, part of
which took the form of prepared statements that Hocker read to
those present. As the circumstances surrounding the crime unfolded,
it transpired that De La Rue and Hocker, a fellow teacher, were
friends who frequently went out to 'court' women. A year earlier
Hocker had introduced his friend to a 'beautiful young lady of
Hampstead', the mysterious Caroline! Hocker had designs on the
woman himself but De La Rue made a greater impression and,
according to the prisoner, allowed herself to be seduced by him. As
a result, Hocker argued that Caroline's parents and brother sought
revenge and asked him to help. He confessed to writing the letter
'signed Caroline' to lure De La Rue to an appointed spot whereupon
her brother would seek vengeance upon her seducer. Hocker stated
that he accompanied the fraternal avenger part of the way and then
left him to go on alone whilst he (Hocker) waited at the *Swiss Cottage*
tavern. It was the cries of murder that alerted him to where he found
Police Constable Baldock with the deceased. Following the
encounter, he returned to the tavern. A waiter at the hostelry attested
that he saw Hocker taking brandy but did not notice any traces of
blood on his clothing; it was revealed that he wore multi-layers that
evening. Nonsensically, Hocker refused to divulge the identity of
Caroline's brother or that of the family name. Was this out of a
misplaced sense of loyalty? Or, more so, because there was simply no
family seeking revenge at all! A man in Hocker's position would
surely call upon these persons for corroboration of his story. In
trying to account for the bloodstains on his clothes found at his
home, he bizarrely explained that, later in the evening, he visited the
family's home in Hampstead to look for the alleged killer. As he was
the principal cause of the tragedy, and in order to distract suspicion
away from the brother, Hocker decided to visit a nearby
slaughterhouse. Here, he 'disfigured his clothes in a pool of blood
which I found handy.' Poor Thomas could not even convincingly
perjure his way out of the desperate situation in which he now found
himself. As to the charge of theft, Hocker again denied this, asserting
that the deceased had given the money to him on the morning of the
murder, as with the watch and ring, which De La Rue had left with
him to get repaired. Yet, once again, no one could substantiate this

explanation. To all concerned, it was clear that his motives for murder were jealously and petty gain and his version of events pure fantasy.

After Mr Justice Coleman summed up the evidence, in a trial that lasted less than ten hours, the jury retired to consider a verdict. They returned just ten minutes later, and not surprisingly, Thomas Hocker was found guilty on all counts. Until his execution on 28 April, only days before his twenty-second birthday, the prisoner took up residence in the condemned cell at Newgate Prison. Hocker continued to protest his innocence blaming a second party who he would not name, declaring, 'Let, then, this sentence ring in the murderer's ears: That he is not only the destroyer of De La Rue, but of me likewise. I did not lift a hand against the deceased!'

Hocker's execution was no less dramatic than events surrounding the crime itself. By early morning, up to 10,000 people had assembled outside Debtor's Door at Newgate to watch the hanging scheduled for 8 am. Twenty minutes before, Hocker twice fainted and his whole frame became prostrated. He was placed in a chair, carried from his cell into the open air and then, 'by the aid of common restoratives ... and by artificial means, the unhappy criminal was resuscitated from a state resembling death only to undergo death in its reality.' With the help of the assistant hangman, the prisoner was lifted to his feet and the noose placed around his neck by executioner William Calcraft. Thomas Hocker was heard to have asked God to receive his soul and, with that, he dropped through the trap door and into the hereafter, his 'animal propensity' doubtless sated for all eternity.

# CHAPTER 10

# Death in 'Little Italy':
# The Saffron Hill Murder
# 1864

*The Italian's fate appeared sealed or so it seemed.*

s thirty-eight-year-old costermonger Michael Harrington lay dying in St Bartholomew's Hospital, as result of a fatal stab wound to the stomach, the police brought his alleged attacker to his bedside. Witnessed by Inspector Thomas Potter and Police Constable Richard Fawell, the victim made the following statement:

*St Bartholomew's Hospital where dying stab victim Michael Harrington wrongly identified Seraphino Pelizzioni, an Italian glass worker, as his attacker.*

*My name is Michael Harrington. I was at the Golden Anchor public house, Great Saffron-hill, about seven o'clock this evening. I was stabbed in the belly. The man with a moustache is the man that did it. God forgive him. I mean the man now present. I am on my dying bed. God forgive him … St. Bartholomew's Hospital, Dec. 26 [1864].*

Having made this accusation, Harrington died the following morning from his injuries. The moustached man in question was Seraphino Pelizzioni (aka Polioni), a thirty-three-year-old Italian glass silverer of Clerkenwell. The two policemen then marched Pelizzioni to the Royal Free Hospital where twenty-two-year-old Alfred Rebbeck, pot man at

*Ordnance Survey Map of 1872 showing the* Golden Anchor *public house on the corner of Great Saffron Hill and Castle Street (now Saffron Street).*

the *Golden Anchor*, also lay suffering from a knife wound. He too gave a statement identifying the Italian as his attacker, 'there was a disturbance at the Anchor, Great Saffron-hill. I went into to try to quell it … This statement is true … The man that stabbed me is now present. That is the man.' A third man was also cut in the disturbance. Charles Bannister received a serious gash to one of his hands and consequently lost part of a finger; Pelizzioni again was identified as the perpetrator. The Italian's fate appeared sealed or so it seemed. In a case underpinned by cultural antagonism, conflicting evidence and mistaken identity, the truth eventually emerged but not before an innocent man was sentenced to death for a crime he did not commit.

The labyrinthine streets surrounding Saffron Hill and Hatton Garden were home to an increasing number of Italian immigrants. Together with a maze of streets to the north of adjoining Clerkenwell Road, the area later became known as 'Little Italy'. On Boxing Day 1864, a group of men including Michael Harrington met to have a post-Christmas drink in the *Anchor's* bagatelle room, which was connected to the tap-room by a short passageway. The pub itself was located at 59 Great Saffron Hill, now the site of a modern apartment block on the corner of Saffron Hill and Saffron Street, Holborn. At around 7 pm, the atmosphere in the hostelry exploded when a moustached Italian, accompanied by a number of compatriots, entered the bagatelle room. A brawl ensued, resulting in Harrington, Rebbeck and Bannister being stabbed, allegedly by the be-whiskered Italian. Identified as Seraphino Pelizzioni, the Italian was taken to the local police station whilst the wounded were treated at the aforementioned hospitals. Following the death of Harrington, the case became one of murder. Many witnesses attested that Pelizzioni was definitely the frenzied knife-wielding aggressor and that his motive for attack was one of revenge against the pub's landlord, Frederick Shaw. There can be little doubt either that all parties involved had their 'national sensibilities' heightened by over consumption of alcohol!

With Pelizzioni arrested for murder, the magistrate's hearing began at Clerkenwell Police Court, King's Cross Road, on 27 December. Amongst those giving evidence was Shaw, who described how he had been earlier struck by an Italian, after which a row ensued. The landlord then explained how he had gone for the police and, on his return, discovered that Pelizzioni had attacked three men. The series of events leading up to the Italian's arrest was corroborated by a number of indigenous witness accounts at the scene but, alarmingly, no eyewitness statements were taken from the Italian contingent present. Throughout the following January, Mr Knox, the magistrate, examined the evidence, during which the accused was defended by barrister Mr Lewis through an official interpreter, Mr Guerini. One of the main witnesses for the prosecution was Alfred Rebbeck who, although still weakened by his ordeal, had recovered enough give his account:

> *On the night of the 26th ult. I saw about 12 or 14 Italians coming into the bagatelle-room, Seraphino leading. I had been in there, and was coming away from the bar when I saw them. I was returning with a pipe. I saw one of the men knock down a woman. It was not Seraphino who did that. I then hallooed out, 'No row here.' I was at the door. I then saw the prisoner Seraphino stab me in the right side. I saw him pull the knife out of me. It was covered with blood. I am certain that it was Seraphino who did it, as I have known him for the past five or six years. I then struck him with the broom-handle. He made a run at me and made another hit, but I slipped on one side. I saw the knife in his hand a second time. I put my hand to my side where I was stabbed. This was all in the bagatelle-room. I heard an exclamation in the room, and turned my head. I then saw the prisoner and Harrington fall together. I went over with the broom-handle in my hand. Someone took it away, but I do not know who did so. I took hold of the prisoner by the collar, and fell on my knees. I wanted to pull him off.*

After the considering the evidence, Mr Knox committed Pelizzioni for trial for the wilful murder of Harrington. With no respite from his accusers, the Italian now faced examination over his alleged stabbing of Rebbeck. Seraphino vehemently protested that it was not he that wielded the knife against Michael Harrington or Alfred Rebbeck. Yet, eyewitness testimony appeared to contradict his plea of innocence. Pub customer John Liddell, a french polisher of Gray's Inn, confirmed Rebbeck's earlier statement, as did Constable Fawell from the point at which he arrived on the scene. Other victim, Charles Bannister of Back Hill, Holborn, described how, in the affray, he was stabbed in the hand and consequently lost part of his little finger. Bannister's story was backed by George Stanley, of Chapel Street, who witnessed Pelizzioni push through the large crowd of English and Italians in an attempt to leave the pub and in doing so caught Bannister with a knife; the Italian strongly denied possessing such a weapon. It was Stanley who then felled Seraphino shortly after, 'I immediately struck Pelizzioni on the head with a stick, and he fell over Harrington, and that is the way that the prisoner got on top of the deceased.' Finding there to be sufficient proof, the magistrate once more committed the Italian to the Central Criminal Court in Old Bailey, this time to face the charge of the attempted murder of Alfred Rebbeck.

The Court Recorder read out the indictment for murder against Pelizzioni to the jury on 30 January 1865 and his trial began a few days later on 3 February. Accompanied by Mr Ribton, Lewis returned again to defend the Italian. Spectators in court included the much respected Mr Henry Negretti (of Negretti and Zampa, optical and scientific instrument makers) and other leading members of the Italian community in London. Seraphino Pelizzioni elected to be tried by an English jury and, when asked, pleaded not guilty to murdering Harrington. The first witness for the prosecution was Fred Shaw. He repeated his earlier statement, adding, 'I and my wife were in the bar and he [Pelizzioni] said he could kill any six Englishmen like me. I took no notice of the remark.' Shaw further mentioned that, after the threat, Pelizzioni left but there were still many other 'foreigners' in the tap-room. This included a man named Gregorio who was to then to strike the landlord in the mouth. Naturally, a commotion ensued and Shaw left to fetch a policeman. Again, John Liddell gave witness. He informed the court that there was much confusion in the tap-room that threatened to escalate. Many other witnesses that appeared at the earlier magistrate's hearing also repeated their testaments, each story remaining constant.

In Pelizzioni's defence, Mr Ribton suggested that,

*the prisoner was not the man by whom the blow was struck which caused the death of the deceased. This should be proved by reliable testimony. The identification rested entirely on the testimony of partisan witnesses, whose account of such a transaction could not be relied upon. It was clear that, on the night of the murder, there had been a regular party fight, a national quarrel, and it was most improbable that they should have a true account.*

To counter the somewhat Anglo-centric bias of witness testimony, the barrister called for an Italian account of events. In doing so, he shed further doubt upon Pelizzioni's guilt. For the first time in evidence a new suspect was introduced to the proceedings, namely Gregorio Mogni, a forty-one-year-old Italian picture frame maker. Rocco Angelinetta, of St John's Street, Clerkenwell, took to the witness box. Being Mogni's employer and landlord, he said that his employee did not arrive home after the event and, furthermore, he resembled Pelizzioni in appearance; he too wore 'whiskers' and knew the prisoner. Gasperie Massi and other Italian drinkers present at the *Golden Anchor* confirmed the resemblance, and Pietro Marrazi attested that Mogni also had a knife with him. Judge Mr Baron Martin summoned up the evidence at the end of the nine hour trial and, dismissing the introduction of another suspect, informed the jury that 'the evidence was about the clearest and the most direct that, after a long course of experience in the administration of criminal justice, I have ever seen.' Whether Baron Martin was made to retract his words when, a few months later, the case was re-examined was never reported but, for the present, and undoubtedly influenced by his lordship's emphatic statement, the members of the jury took just fifteen minutes to find Seraphino guilty as charged. Only one sentence could be passed and, upon donning a black cap, the judge decreed that the unfortunate Italian was to be hanged by the neck until he was dead.

Less than a week had passed since sentencing when the convicted Pelizzioni heard news of a possible reprieve. The news came following a full confession, as to the stabbing of Harrington, by Gregorio Mogni. It transpired that Mogni was in fact a cousin of Pelizzioni, hence their physical similarity. He had fled to Birmingham but was persuaded back to London by Henry Negretti to face charges. Accompanied to King's Cross Police Station by Negretti, Gregorio was charged on his own confession with having committed the murder; a stay of execution was later granted to Seraphino. Indicted for wilful murder on 27 February, Gregorio Mogni stood trial soon after. As the original witnesses could not be called upon to re-testify, the trial jury's decision would therefore be solely reliant upon new evidence. The case attracted great public interest, especially given that Mogni argued that he only used the knife in self-defence and it was never his intention that anyone should die in the mêlée. Gregorio Mogni also swore that Seraphino arrived at the *Golden Anchor* from a nearby pub, the *Three Tuns* in Cross Street, purely to act as peacemaker between the two warring factions. Additional evidence was forwarded by a relative of Harrington, Mr Worms, who on the night of the stabbing informed police that Mogni was the real culprit not Pelizzioni but was ignored. It can only be assumed that detectives suppressed this vital piece of evidence as admission to a wrongful arrest may have brought discredit to the force! Eventually, justice was to prevail. Gregorio Mogni was found guilty not of murder but of manslaughter, a crime for which he was awarded five years imprisonment with hard labour.

Pelizzioni was not quite in the clear, as the matter of the attempted murder of Rebbeck was yet to be addressed. For total acquittal, the innocent Italian needed to be found not guilty of this charge too. So, on 15 April 1865, he appeared at the Central Criminal Court to face his peers once more. On hand again for Seraphino were Messrs Ribton and Lewis. Witness after witness came forward to give their account of the event. Again, such was the interest in the proceedings, the public gallery was described as being 'one in appearance of the worse parts of a theatre.' Onlookers included the Marquis d'Azeglio, the Italian Ambassador, sheriffs and under-sheriffs and several aldermen. Following the judge's summing up at the end of the trial, the jury retired for just ten minutes and its foreman returned the popular verdict of not guilty! The crowded courtroom and gallery rejoiced. It was noted that even the Marquis appeared to share in the general joy but took care to 'evince his gratification with proper decorum.' Seraphino Pelizzioni was now exonerated from all charges. The authorities granted him a free pardon and sanctioned his immediate release.

As to the state of Anglo-Italian relationships, following the acquittal, little is recorded but, for the next fifty years, 'Little Italy' grew into a thriving and respected community. It would be encouraging to think that, out of this Boxing Day tragedy, the Holborn citizens of both nations experienced a greater camaraderie, thus enabling each to share in the economic prosperity which the latter half of the nineteenth century brought to many in the area.

# CHAPTER 11

# The Bloomsbury and Euston Murder Mysteries 1872–84

*She was lying dead on her back, in a pool of blood …*

Between 1872 and 1884, four murders occurred in the St Pancras area of north Bloomsbury and Euston, with two of these taking place just a few doors apart in the same street. Elevating this quartet of crime above the norm is the singular fact that no persons were ever found guilty of the killings. To this day, true identities and motives behind the slayings remain securely buried with the corpses of the four female victims.

The first of these mysteries happened early on Christmas Day 1872. Twenty-seven-year-old theatre worker and part-time prostitute, Harriet Buswell (aka Clara Burton), occupied a second floor back room at 12 Great Coram Street (now Coram Street), Bloomsbury. Later that festive day, landlady Mrs Harriet Wright thought her tenant's absence unusual and, suspecting something amiss, had Miss Buswell's door broken open. Upon entering, a shocking sight was beheld. Her tenant was found to be quite dead, her throat having been severely cut. *The Times* (27 December 1872) gave a graphic account of the injuries, describing how 'the murderer stabbed the poor girl under her left ear [with] another wound on the left of the wind-pipe large enough to put a man's fist in.' Harriet Buswell's door had been locked on the outside and the key removed. A few trinkets and the victim's purse were also missing from the room. It was speculated that 'the murderer might have supposed that a person living in so respectable a locality would have some booty, hence the crime.' The coroner's inquest took place on 27 December, with Mrs Wright giving a lengthy account of her murdered tenant's character. She also testified that she saw a stranger with the victim late on Christmas Eve and was informed that he would be staying the night. Her description of the stranger, now the prime suspect, soon appeared on official police notices, together with an announcement of £100 reward for anyone with information leading to a conviction:

*Age 25, height 5' 9", complexion swarthy, red spots on face, black hair, no whiskers or moustache, but not shaved for two or three days, stout build, dress dark, tight fitting coat, dark billycock hat, a foreigner (supposed German).*

*12 Great Coram Street (right), c.1920s. The house was the scene of a Christmas Day murder in 1872. The building no longer exists.*

It may have been the handsome incentive, or even a xenophobic opportunity to 'finger a foreigner', that led some to come forward with the names of a few Teutonic suspects. Police also alerted railway stations and ports and, amongst the first to be apprehended, in what was to become a wave of wrongful arrests, was a German attempting to board a North Sea ferry at Harwich bound for Rotterdam. Justifiably released, another fellow countryman was then mistakenly identified as a potential suspect. Leading the investigation was Superintendent Thomas. He had his sights firmly upon a German clergyman named Dr Hessel. It transpired that the doctor and his wife were in London for a week, whilst his ship was in repair at Ramsgate. He was allegedly seen by witnesses in the company of the victim prior to the event but these accusations could not be substantiated and Hessel was released. The police were at loss and continued to investigate new sightings of the suspect, all of which came to a dead end. As late as July 1873, the force was still on the lookout for foreign suspects, even as far afield as Ireland. In connection with this, a letter from Enniskillen was published in *The Times* for 25 July 1873. Written by a German citizen on a walking tour, he had been held for twenty-four hours in regard to the Christmas murder. Disgruntled at being treated 'all that fearful time almost like a convicted murderer,' the rambler was released after evidence proving his innocence arrived from England. His letter was signed, 'Another arrested German'.

It was evident by now the perpetrator had slipped the police net. The motive for murder was also unclear. What had seemed like an opportunist robbery was clearly something more sinister. Could this have been a murder for sexual gratification? Or, perhaps, it was the end result of an argument that went hideously wrong, with the stealing of a few possessions a cover up for these two possibilities. Speculation aside, the crime remained unsolved and the murderer of poor Harriet Buswell never found. Her case, however, was not to stay unique to the area for long. Just seven years later another murder occurred nearby that also confounded the authorities.

About five minutes walk to the north of Great Coram Street lay Burton Crescent. Today, this leafy locale is known as Cartwright Gardens but, in December 1878, the street gained notoriety due to the grisly murder of seventy-four-year old Rachel Samuels. The widow of a diamond merchant, Mrs Samuels lived at 4 Burton Crescent, which stood on the eastern side of the street; London University halls of residence now occupy the site. Another resident of the house was a French musician, Mr Birschystryky, and it was he that discovered the body of the old lady in the early hours of 12 December. Returning from

*4 Burton Crescent, 1903. Here, in 1878, seventy-four-year-old Rachel Samuels was murdered. Burton Crescent was renamed Cartwright Gardens in 1908.*

work as a theatre orchestra player, and in search of his supper, the musician found Mrs Samuels in the kitchen. She was lying dead on her back in a pool of blood, with several wounds about her head, hands and feet. The police deduced that Mrs Samuels had been attacked earlier that evening with,

> *a heavy piece of wood, studded with nails, that had formed part of a hat-rail; and several blows with this dangerous weapon must have been struck, as the poor woman's hands were cut to pieces, as though she had endeavoured to protect her head and body.*

Evidently, the victim's house showed no sign of violent entry and therefore the investigators decided that Mrs Samuels must have known her attacker. It was further noted that nothing had seemingly been removed or disturbed and thus the crime was not, as first believed, 'the offspring of a premeditated robbery.'

It was not long until a suspect was arrested for this somewhat cowardly crime. A former servant to the victim, Mary Donovan, was charged and appeared at Bow Street Magistrates' Court. In attempting to explain the circumstantial evidence against her, Mary protested her innocence throughout the hearing. Although not being in the permanent employ of Mrs Samuels, the accused continued to visit the old lady and would occasionally act as her charwoman. It was proved that, on 11 December, she had visited number 4 Burton Crescent and had stayed as late as 8.30 pm. Mary did not return home but instead had gone to sleep in a nearby coffee shop, as she could not rouse anyone at home; her husband was a night watchman. She also had blood on her clothing and was found wearing a pair of boots once belonging to Mrs Samuels. The bloodstains, however, were too few and too slight to be conclusive and she claimed that her husband bought her the boots, a fact that he declined to confirm. Her explanation was hastily ignored by police, who were doubtless looking for an early conviction. With robbery as possible motive, Mary was charged with wilful murder but she was not to remain in custody for long. On 10 January 1879, at Bow Street Magistrates Court, and with the solely circumstantial evidence insufficient to commit her to trial, the case against the former servant came to an impotent conclusion and she was free to walk. Undoubtedly, many associated with the case continued to believe in Mary Donovan's guilt and she herself would carry that burden of suspicion for the rest of her life. What was reassuring about Mary's acquittal though was the advancement that jurisprudence had made by this time. Here, a comparison can be made with the earlier

*4 Euston Square. In 1879, the decomposed remains of Matilda Hacker were found in the building's cellar after her disappearance from the dwelling eighteen months later. The bus terminus at Euston Station now occupies the site.*

case of poor Eliza Fenning who, in 1815, was hanged following a conviction based upon the weakest of circumstantial evidence. If tried sixty-four years later, Eliza's case would have been almost certainly dismissed (see Chapter 7). This, of course, would have been of little comfort to the relatives and friends of Rachel Samuels. Their disappointment over not securing the conviction of the person or persons responsible for her death was doubtless shared by those associated with another unsolved killing revealed just six months later. This proved to be a similar case involving another aged female and, as before, the charge of murder against the prime suspect was dismissed due to poor circumstantial evidence.

In 1879, residential Euston Square could be found a few hundred metres to the north-west of Burton Crescent; then, the square traversed both sides of Euston Road, adjacent to St Pancras (New) Church. Today, the square still exists but is now a largely grassed area located between Euston Road and the forecourt to Euston Station. 4 Euston

*Miss Matilda Hacker. Her murder remains unsolved.*

MISS HACKER. FROM A PHOTO.

Square could be found on the north side near the junction with
Seymour Street, now Eversholt Street. It was the home of Sewerin and
Mary Bastendorff and family and a number of lodgers, including sixty-
year-old Matilda Hacker. Miss Hacker took up residency at the address
in late September 1877 but disappeared midway through the following
month, leaving no forwarding address. Her disappearance initially
puzzled the Bastendorffs but after a while the household continued
about its everyday business. Indeed, no more was thought of the matter
until eighteen months later when, on 9 May 1879, the decaying remains
of an elderly lady were unexpectedly discovered in the lodging house's
coal cellar (see Back Cover). A boy employed at the house, William
Strohman, was ordered to clear out the cellar, as it had not been used
for some time. In the darkest corner he came across some jewellery and
female clothing and finally the decomposed body covered in layers of
coal dust. It was later confirmed that these were indeed the remains of
Matilda Hacker. Foul play was immediately suspected and proved

*Miss Hannah Dobbs, 1879. She was acquitted of the murder of Matilda Hacker.*

HANNAH DOBBS FROM A SKETCH IN COURT.

when, on inspection, traces of rope or cord were found deeply embedded in the deceased's neck. Detailed examination of the body was to show that death was caused by strangulation.

It was established that the victim was still alive on 10 October 1877, as she had written and posted a letter dated thus. A few days later, twenty-four-year-old servant Hannah Dobbs, who had been attending to the needs of Miss Hacker, was ordered by Mrs Bastendorff to fetch the old lady's rent. As Hannah had conversed with Miss Hacker whilst collecting the payment, the victim was clearly alive at this point but, by 15 October, she had suddenly vacated her rooms without giving any prior notice. A while after Miss Hacker's mysterious departure, it was recalled that Hannah Dobbs had been sighted in possession of a large amount of money – supposedly left to her in a will – along with two watches and a chain, which some believed to be the property of the deceased. Furthermore, the servant retrieved trinkets from a pawnbroker under the pseudonym of Rosina Bastindo; these items were also alleged to be the property of Matilda Hacker. After discovery of the remains and the subsequent investigation of events of eighteen months earlier, Hannah Dobbs was duly arrested for the wilful murder of Miss Hacker.

Hannah left the employ of the Bastendorffs in September 1878 but remained a frequent visitor to their house. It was intimated that she had enjoyed a personal relationship with Sewerin Bastendorff and then later kept company with his brother, Peter. Hannah's trial began on 2 July 1879 at the Central Criminal Court, Old Bailey. Pleading not guilty in a firm voice, the prisoner was attired in a black cotton dress and betrayed no signs of anxiety in respect to the proceedings. One of the chief witnesses was Mary Bastendorff who attested that she often saw Hannah wear jewellery that looked very similar to that once worn by Matilda Hacker. Perhaps Mrs Bastendorff saw this as an opportunity to avenge her former servant's supposed indiscretion with her husband. Hannah explained that the items of jewellery were, in fact, given to her by an uncle. The trial lasted two days and contained more contradictory facts than confirmed truths, many of these initiated by Sewerin Bastendorff. Mr Justice Hawkins took over two hours to sum up the facts to the members of the jury who, in turn, took just thirty minutes to find Hannah Dobbs not guilty of murdering Miss Hacker. What was known during the early summer of 1879 as the 'Euston Square Murder' became forever known as 'the Euston Square Mystery'. As in the Samuel's case, the jury had no alternative than to acquit, and once again justice prevailed. The trial of Hannah Dobbs proved that there was not one shred of direct evidence to convict her,

# "POLICE NEWS" EDITION.
# THE EUSTON SQUARE MYSTERY.
## EXTRAORDINARY STATEMENT MADE BY
# HANNAH DOBBS

CONTAINING

HER LIFE AND EARLY CAREER — HISTORY OF MISS HACKER
WHILE IN EUSTON SQUARE—HARROWING DETAILS—
STORY OF THE MURDER, &c., &c.

PORTRAIT OF HANNAH DOBBS.

## PRICE ONE PENNY.

G. PURKESS, 286, STRAND, LONDON, W.C.

*Hannah Dobbs' story. The booklet's revelations led to the conviction of her former employer, Mr Sewerin Bastendorff, for perjury during her trial.*

and even the broadsheet press condemned the evidence presented by the prosecution as being extremely weak. In an attempt to redress trial inaccuracies, Hannah boldly published a booklet detailing the full history of the case. Her revelations caused such a stir that, following investigation, Sewerin Bastendorff was found guilty of perjury during her trial. In spite of Hannah's best selling version of events exonerating her in the affair, she doubtless carried around the stigma of guilt by association for her remaining days, whilst the real killer(s) remained free for the rest of theirs.

Remaining also unidentified and at large was the perpetrator of the final murder in this quartet of unsolved mysteries. Attracting much tabloid coverage was the brutal killing of nineteen-year-old Mary Ann Yates at 12 Burton Crescent. The street once again became the centre of morbid attention when, on the morning of Sunday, 9 March 1884, and only doors away from the house in which Rachel Samuels was

*A dramatic picture published in the* Illustrated Police News, *30 March 1884, depicting the discovery of the grisly murder of Mary Ann Yates at 12 Burton Crescent.*

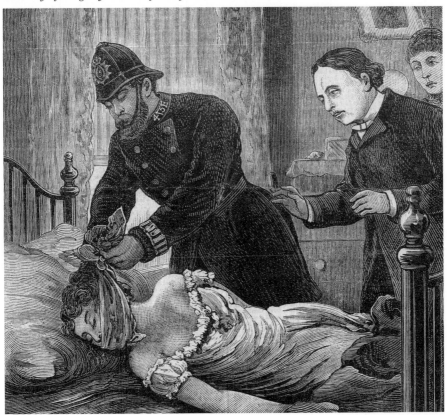

murdered six years earlier, the young female was found dead in bed. According to *The Times* (11 March 1884), she was discovered 'with her head on the pillow in a pool of blood, which had issue from a serious gash on the left side of her head, above the ear, while a towel was tied tightly over her mouth, the knot being at the back.' The coroner's jury later decided that 'the deceased died from the mortal effects of suffocation by strangulation, caused by a towel being placed around the neck by some man at present unknown, who was thereby guilty of murder.' The usual reward of £100 was offered for information leading to the arrest of the killer. Mary was known to have been a prostitute plying her trade from the premises. Her early life had been a sad one too. Suffering from partial paralysis and having spent her childhood days in Westminster Workhouse and then Tooting Industrial School, she later found employment as nurse-girl and servant at various London addresses. These positions were often short-lived and eventually Mary found herself 'working the streets' around St Pancras.

It was in the small hours of 9 March 1884 that Mary attended her final client. She had stepped out earlier that evening with fellow lodger and friend Annie Ellis. At approximately 1 am, the two friends had just parted company when Mary fell into conversation with a smartly dressed gentleman in Euston Road. Less than an hour later, witnesses heard Mary return home accompanied by a heavily foot-stepped man. At around 3 am, lodgers adjacent to the young prostitute heard screams coming from her room. They chose to ignore the commotion, as Mary was apparently prone to fits of hysteria and often made such noises. A while after the disturbances had died down, witnesses again heard the footsteps of a man descend the lodging's stairs and go out through the front door. This too was a common occurrence and, once more, no notice was taken of the departing stranger. Later on, Annie Ellis found it peculiar that Mary had not attended breakfast, so around midday she decided to see if all was well with her friend. It was then that the terrible sight of her murdered friend presented itself.

The coroner's inquest into the death was held on 12 March at Crowndale Hall, St Pancras, with Dr Danford Thomas presiding. Evidence from Professor Augustus Pepper indicated that, owing to the nature of the bruising found on her body, brave Mary had put up a strong struggle before succumbing to her killer's will. Apart from the medical findings, very little information of use to the police was forthcoming. One of Mary's bags was found empty with an open rip along one side and a ring worn regularly by Mary was missing, but these provided no further clues. Motive for the attack also remained speculative; petty robbery or an argument over 'service' charges were just two of the suggestions forwarded. Attempts by detectives to trace the gentleman visitor proved negative and the tragic end to Mary's sad life was never avenged. Her final resting place became St Pancras Cemetery, East Finchley. In a touching gesture, Annie Ellis and a few friends offered to cover the cost of interment rather than allow the parish to bear the expense. The few articles left by Mary were, at the coroner's behest, given to Annie who had borne the greater share of funeral expenses.

With its decline from Regency prosperity to late Victorian notoriety, Burton Crescent was given a chance to eradicate its 'homicidal' reputation. In 1908, St Pancras councillors saw fit to change the street's name to Cartwright Gardens, after John Cartwright, political reformer and former resident of the street. Meanwhile, the Mary Ann Yates case joined the trio of earlier, unsolved murders; each now immortalised within the area's darker history.

# CHAPTER 12

# A Carriage of Convenience: The Case of Mary Pearcey and the Hoggs of Kentish Town 1890

*Upon entering the road he noticed the motionless body of a woman slumped on the ground ...*

Can murder run in a family? Although there is no conclusive evidence to back such a theory, discussion about this would have almost certainly taken place back in 1890 to suggest that such a phenomena could very well occur. On 23 December 1890, twenty-four-year-old Mary Eleanor Pearcey (née Wheeler) was hanged for the murders of Phoebe Hogg and her baby daughter, also named Phoebe. Mary's execution took place just ten years after her father's hanging at St Albans Prison in November 1880. Thomas Wheeler was convicted for the murder of a Hertfordshire farmer. Whilst awaiting execution, Wheeler wrote to his victim's widow apologising for his crime. Furthermore, he asked her forgiveness and prayed that his own wife and daughters, including a then fourteen-year-old Mary, would not pay for his sinful crime. Despite this eleventh hour act of contrition, the murderer's prayers were not answered and Mary was destined to follow her father to the gallows.

During her late teens, Mary enjoyed a brief relationship with John Pearcey, a carpenter. Although the couple never married, Mary took his surname as her own and, despite parting company, she continued to adopt Pearcey in place of Wheeler; this may have been an attempt to disassociate herself from her father's crime. She was not an outstanding beauty but, with russet hair and blue eyes, young Mary did not encounter any difficulty in attracting male admirers. In about 1888, one of these, Charles Creighton of Gravesend, arranged rooms for her at 2 Priory Street (now Ivor Street), located at the southern end of Kentish Town. He would visit Mary most Fridays to 'avail' of her company. Meanwhile, Mary had also caught the roving eye of local furniture remover and married man, Frank Samuel Hogg. Conveniently, Frank lived at 141 Prince of Wales Road, Kentish Town, a mere ten-minute walk from Mary's house. His philandering with Mary had begun before his wedding to thirty-year-old Phoebe Styles in November 1888 and continued afterwards. At the time of marriage, Phoebe was also three months pregnant with their daughter and, following the birth, she became unwell. Early in 1890, Frank employed Mary to nurse his wife and to look after baby Phoebe. Despite a fear that Mrs Hogg had over her husband being 'intimate' with the new home help, the two women attempted to socialise. It was on one such social occasion that events were triggered, the like of which Kentish Town and parts of neighbouring Hampstead had never before witnessed.

At 11 am on Friday, 24 October 1890, Mary gave a young boy named William Holmes a penny to carry a note to Phoebe Hogg inviting her for tea that afternoon. Phoebe accepted the invitation and, a little after 3 pm, set out with her baby for Priory Street. Half an hour on and Phoebe was seen knocking at Mary's door by

*Mary Eleanor Pearcey. Like father, like daughter: Pearcey was hanged for double murder ten years after her father's execution, Thomas Wheeler, also hanged for murder. Portrait drawn by Rachel Dilworth from a contemporary pamphlet.*

Charles Britt, a carman with stables in nearby Priory Mews (later Priory Place, now Prowse Place). He also noticed a large bassinette perambulator (pram) parked outside on the pavement. Apart from the murderer, this was the last time that anyone saw Phoebe Hogg alive. Thirty minutes later, next-door neighbour, Charlotte Pridington, heard the sound of breaking glass coming from Mary's rooms. Duly concerned, Mrs Pridington called over the adjoining fence to ensure that all was well but received no reply.

A few hours later, at approximately 7 pm, Mr S MacDonald, a young clerk, was returning home to Belsize Park, Hampstead. His journey took him along Crossfield Road, then a small, dark and partially built

*Ordnance Survey map of 1894 showing Priory Street (now Ivor Street), Kentish Town. Mary Pearcey's house at 2 Priory Street was located on the north side of the street a few doors down from the* Old Eagle *public house at 251 Great College Street.*

thoroughfare running north from Eton Avenue near Swiss Cottage. Upon entering the road he noticed the motionless body of a woman slumped on the ground and whose head was wrapped with clothing. Believing that she was inebriated, Mr MacDonald ignored the situation and walked on. Then, thinking that she may perhaps be ill and require assistance, he paused and decided to retrace his steps towards the woman. He found to his horror that the poor female, in fact, appeared to be dead. At the nearby *Swiss Cottage* tavern, he informed Police Constable Gardiner of his discovery. On reaching Crossfield Road, the policeman began to unwrap what appeared to be a man's sleeveless cardigan from around the head of the woman. The unravelling of the garment revealed a grisly sight. An article in the *Hampstead and Highgate Express* (25 October 1890) noted that, 'Her throat, it was seen, had been so severely cut by some extremely sharp instrument that both the windpipe and the spinal column had been divided, and the head almost severed from the body.' It was also reported that the poor victim's face was extremely battered and bruised. Given the brutality of the attack, the newspapers theorised that 'Jack the Ripper' himself had returned, transferring his attentions from Whitechapel to Hampstead. It was quickly deduced that, as there was relatively little blood and no murder weapon found at the scene, the killing took place elsewhere; Crossfield Road was merely a convenient location for the murderer to dispose of the body. The victim's pockets were searched for identity but none could be found. Discovered by the corpse, however, was an iron nut. This proved to belong to a bloodstained perambulator found abandoned some distance away in Hamilton Terrace, St John's Wood. It appeared that the carriage was earlier used to transport the body, as hair found stuck inside the pram matched that of the victim's. A while later, Gipsy Smith, who had an encampment at Swiss Cottage, found the dead body of an infant at the side of Finchley Road. Apart from a few minor cuts and bruises to its face, the child appeared to have suffocated.

Meanwhile, Frank Hogg had returned home late from work to find his wife and daughter absent. He was not overly concerned and thought that Phoebe may have gone to visit her parents in Rickmansworth or her brothers in Chorleywood. The following day, however, Frank became worried, especially as reports of the crime began to filter through along with descriptions of the deceased. By evening, the now distraught husband reported his wife missing and dispatched his sister, Clara Hogg, and a reluctant Mary Pearcey to St Pancras Mortuary to identify the victim's body. Upon arrival at the mortuary, Mary attempted to prevent Frank's sister from viewing the remains but a determined Clara made a positive identification; the body was indeed that of Phoebe Hogg. At this point, and having seen the extent of Phoebe's injuries, Mary became hysterical. The two were also invited to identify the pram found in St John's Wood. This too was confirmed as belonging to Mrs Hogg. A Priory Street resident later informed police that she had seen Mary wheeling the heavily laden pram on the evening of the murder.

In the ensuing police investigation, headed by Detective Inspector Bannister, Frank Hogg, now a potential suspect, was questioned and his house in Prince of Wales Road searched. He gave full details as to his movements on 24 October and, now full of remorse, admitted his affair with Mary Pearcey but denied murdering his wife. Given her duplicity with Frank and her performance in the mortuary, the investigators next visited Priory Street to interrogate Mary over the matter. Bannister and his men undertook a thorough search of Mary's rooms, during which they noticed that the kitchen was splashed with blood and its window panes broken. There also appeared to be a recent but ineffectual attempt to clean blood from a carpet, and further searching uncovered a blood soaked carving knife and fire poker. Clearly, a violent struggle of some sort had taken place. During the search, the police experienced Mary's behaviour become somewhat strange. She had taken to the piano and serenaded the officers and when questioned about the bloodstains she replied that she had been, 'killing mice, killing mice, killing mice.' Naturally, Bannister dismissed this excuse. Next, an examination of Mary's clothing revealed bloodstains and, furthermore, one of the wedding rings she wore belonged to Mrs Hogg. Given this initial evidence, Mary Pearcey was arrested for the murder of Phoebe and her infant who, by now, had been identified as Phoebe and Frank's daughter. Following a hearing at Marylebone Police Court, Mary was committed for trial five weeks later. During the committal, she admitted to warder Sarah Sawhill that, during tea on the fateful day, Mrs Hogg had made an offensive remark that resulted in a heated argument. Mary made no further comments to Sawhill, fearing that an explanation of events may only serve to incriminate.

Meanwhile, the funeral of Phoebe and her baby was scheduled to take place on Sunday 3 November. In the pouring rain, nearly 4,000 people had congregated in Camden High Street partly to catch a glimpse of the mournful procession and partly to display their disgust at Frank Hogg's behaviour in the affair. The

*The* Daily Graphic's *portrayal of Mary Pearcey listening to the charges against her at Marylebone Police Court on 28 October 1890.*

*St Pancras Guardian* (8 November 1890) reported that such was the denunciation of the widower that when he first appeared making his way to the first mourning coach there came,

> *a tremendous outburst of violent execrations from the crowd, who also hissed and howled their loudest. They pressed towards the coach with a violence which was for the moment sufficient to overawe the most resolute policeman, but the mounted men from [their position in] Delancey Street speedily rode up and took their positions on each side of the coach and behind, followed by about 100 of the constables on foot, one holding the handle of each of the doors of the carriage.*

*The major players involved in the murders of Phoebe and baby Phoebe Hogg, as depicted in the* Pall Mall Budget, *30 October 1890.*

For practically the entire the route from Camden Town to St Pancras Cemetery at East Finchley, a distance of some eight miles, Frank Hogg met hostility from the crowd, and this was repeated on the return journey. The bodies of his wife and child were interred together in a single coffin. Even at the cemetery some onlookers persisted with their persecution of Frank, with one woman crying out, at the top of her voice, 'Oh you murderer.' Hogg may have been indirectly complicit in his wife's demise but he had not been indicted for her murder. Next, it was towards Mary Pearcey that the mob's interest was to turn.

The trial of Mary Pearcey began at the Central Criminal Court, Old Bailey, on 1 December 1890 and was to last three days. Mary pleaded not guilty; a claim dismissed by the prosecution who proposed that Mary's jealousy of Phoebe was motive for murder. Evidence exposed in detail the relationship Frank Hogg had with Mary before and after his marriage to Phoebe. It appears that, owing to Phoebe's pregnancy, Frank had been forced into matrimony but continued to see Mary on an intimate basis. Initially, Mary accepted this situation and had even befriended Phoebe but having to share Frank was eventually more than she could bear. The physical evidence against Mary also began to mount. The jury listened closely to the circumstances surrounding Mary's actions during the afternoon and evening of the murder, as well as to the details of police findings. Mention was made of the sound of breaking glass emanating from the house, Mary's odd manner in front of the police, her bloodstained clothing, the wearing of Phoebe's wedding ring, witnesses who saw her wheeling the pram and, of course, her strange behaviour at the morgue. Even John Pearcey came forward to testify that the cardigan with which Phoebe's mutilated head was wrapped was one he had previously given Mary. The court also heard how baby Phoebe met her sad end. Her suffocating death, in all probability, caused by the weight of her mother's slain body placed upon her in the pram following the frenzied attack. Mary Pearcey offered no evidence and remained detached throughout the proceedings.

Whether Phoebe's death was premeditated or simply and suddenly, as Mary had earlier intimated, triggered by an ill-timed comment was not determined by the evidence. But, what was determined was her guilt. On the final day of the trial, the jury took just fifty-two minutes to find Mary responsible for the murders. As was customary after the verdict was announced in capital punishment cases, the defendant was invited to say a few words stating why the death penalty should not be awarded. In response, Mary briefly declared only that she was innocent of the crime. After hearing this somewhat unconvincing statement towards her defence, the judge then proceeded to sentence Mary to death by hanging. In an attempt to help explain Mary's murderous actions and earn her a reprieve, Mary's solicitor informed Home Office officials that she may have experienced an epileptic fit just prior to the killing. Mary had suffered from epileptic seizures since early childhood and so, during tea with Phoebe, she may have blacked out and then unconsciously committed the foul deed. This excuse was to have no effect and the date of Mary's execution at Newgate was set for 23 December 1890.

Whilst awaiting her fate, Mary requested that Frank Hogg visit her in prison but he declined. This temporarily upset Mary but otherwise she remained remarkably composed. On her last full day on earth, she summoned her solicitor so that she could put her affairs in order. Bizarrely, Mary also requested that he place a message in the personal column of a Madrid newspaper. This read, 'MECP Last wish of MEW. Have not betrayed. MEW.' Mary chose not to explain the meaning of this cryptic note, nor did she give any other information that might have led to a last minute stay of execution. At 8 am on the day of her hanging, Mary was visited by executioner James Berry. After a brief conversation, followed by the fitting of necessary body straps and belts, Mary made one last statement, 'My sentence is a just one but a good deal of the evidence against me is false.' Is Mary suggesting that, although involved with the crime, another was the real perpetrator? Guarding her secret, Mary was led from the condemned cell and across the yard to the execution shed. From the gallows, a drop of nine feet was prescribed; one foot for every stone of body weight. With final preparations completed, Berry released the lever and Mary Pearcey fell into the hereafter to join her similarly fated father. After hanging for one hour, her body was cut down and later buried in an unmarked grave within the prison.

As for Frank, presumably to avoid the constant recriminations from the local populace, he left Kentish Town to start life anew elsewhere. His parting was no doubt made easier by Madame Tussauds' Waxworks Museum, which gave him £200 for his wife's perambulator and the contents of Mary Pearcey's kitchen. Such was the interest generated by the case that 30,000 people visited Madame Tussauds to view a reconstruction of the murderess's kitchen timed to open on the very day of her execution. Yet, Mary's death left behind a number of unanswered questions that today still remain a mystery. Was the murder a joint conspiracy against Phoebe, with Mary an accessory to murder but not the killer? Was Mary indeed covering for Frank, who decided that life with Phoebe was a mistake? And, intriguingly, what was the meaning of Mary's curious newspaper message? In a case where exceedingly strong circumstantial evidence sealed Mary's fate, answers to these issues were seemingly of no great importance to the authorities. In spite of her relationship with the Hoggs, perhaps Mary's destiny had already been determined at birth. If so, it was only then a matter of when, rather than if, that she would follow in her father's footsteps and succumb to a hereditary predilection to murder!

# CHAPTER 13

# Three's a Crowd: Tragedy in Regent Square
## 1893

*... in a demonstration of public sympathy, nearly 4,000 mourners congregated ...*

Whilst some murder cases are destined to remain unsolved due to lack of suspects, evidence or motive, others fall neatly into the category of 'open and shut'. Nonetheless, these are not without interest. In 1893, one such case featured three persons of respectable background and status involved in a 'love triangle'. The facts leading to the conclusion of this tragic case indicated that there would be only one, inevitable outcome – death.

Ordinarily, Regent Square and its gardens, off Gray's Inn Road, was a quiet, mainly residential location with seemingly little to trouble its everyday existence. Yet, the secluded tranquillity of this St Pancras neighbourhood was violently interrupted when, during the early hours of Thursday, 21 September 1893, three locals were found shot in the north-west corner of the square. The victims were Samuel Barnett Garcia, aged twenty-six, a stock broker of 1 Vernon Chambers, Southampton Row, Leo Eugene Percy, also twenty-six years of age, an electrician and inventor, residing in Swinton Street, St Pancras, and Bessie Constance Montague, a twenty-five-year-old chorus singer, of 18 Regent Square. Three years earlier, Bessie and Leo had enjoyed a long, intimate relationship and were engaged to be married. Unfortunately, the Percy family objected to the match and, with a heavy heart, the young singer dutifully broke off the engagement. This devastated Leo and, rather than looking to the future, he was to remain besotted with his ex-fiancé long after the two had parted company. Bessie kept on friendly terms with Leo but later found another suitor, Samuel Garcia.

Following the 'disengagement', Leo Percy's mood darkened. He became introverted and began to distance himself from his family. By the summer of 1893, according to his brother Cecil, Leo had become 'very strange in his manner, was weak and nervous, and had a curious look about his eyes. He was also very depressed, but was not under medical treatment.' Leo had also taken an overdose of laudanum, originally prescribed for insomnia. Cecil further noticed that his

How the World Wags

**The Regent Square Tragedy** came as a great shock to London and to the general public, proving afresh as it did that the Metropolis is full of romances as sad and as exciting as have ever been chronicled in the annals of fiction. We print on our front page vivid photographs of the exceedingly comely Empire chorus girl, Bessie or "Daisy" Montague, who was shot, with her new lover, by her rejected sweetheart, who then committed suicide.

2. The late Leo Percy.
3. Samuel Garcia.
4. Miss Herbert, "Daisy's" friend.
5. Mrs. Winterbotham, who saw Percy shoot "Daisy," Garcia, and himself.
6. Corner of Regent Square, where the murders and suicide were committed.

*Leo Percy, Samuel Garcia and witnesses from the Regent Square tragedy, as depicted in the* Penny Illustrated Paper, *30 September 1893.*

*Bessie 'Daisy' Montague, a victim of her jilted lover's terrible revenge, as reproduced in the* Penny Illustrated Paper, *30 September 1893.*

brother would sit for hours without speaking, staring at nothing in particular. Little did he know of the dark thoughts and murderous jealousy pervading Leo's mind that were soon to tragically manifest. Meanwhile, under the name 'Daisy' Montague, Bessie continued as a chorus singer, performing now at the *Empire Theatre of Varieties*, Leicester Square. Described as a bright, good-natured church going girl, her relationship with Garcia grew stronger and soon blossomed into an engagement. Her fiancé frequently attended the *Empire* and, happy to be with Bessie whenever possible, he would often arrange to meet her at the stage door in order to escort her home. Leo was also occasionally seen at Bessie's workplace. Although he and Garcia were not formally acquainted, there can be little doubt that the jilted Leo

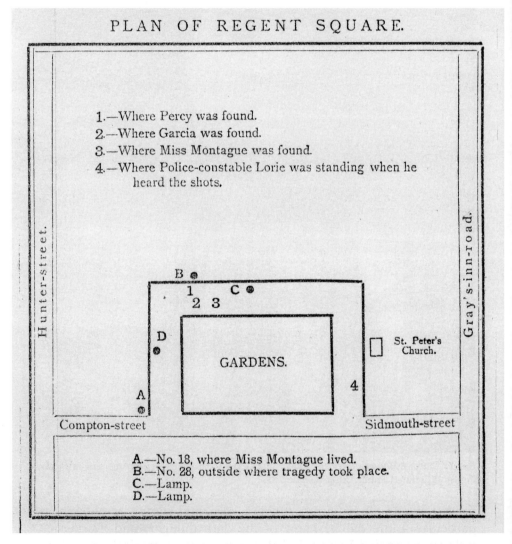

*Plan of Regent Square showing the positions where the tragedy took place. Taken from the* Pall Mall Gazette, *21 September 1893.*

knew about the couple's marital intentions; Bessie may have revealed this to him a few weeks before the impending tragedy, as they were seen arguing.

At 11.30 pm on Wednesday, 20 September, following that evening's performance of *Round the Town*, Bessie and fellow chorus girl and roommate, Augusta Herbert, returned home in the company of Samuel Garcia. The party arrived back in Regent Square at half past midnight. After bidding good night to Miss Herbert, the betrothed couple remained outside and strolled towards St Peter's Church on the east side of the square. Suddenly, according to Miss Herbert, 'she heard a sharp report. That was followed by three other reports.' On leaving her rooms to investigate the sounds, she found a crowd assembled in the street, in the middle of which Miss Montague and two men were lying on the pavement. Bessie was close to the square's garden railings, Garcia a few feet away, and nearby lay Leo Percy with a smoking six-chambered revolver a few inches from his right hand. Evidently, Percy had followed the trio home and, intent on committing a foul deed, hid in a dark corner of Regent Square until a chance for action presented itself. The three bodies were taken to the Royal Free Hospital, Gray's Inn Road, where Bessie and her fiancé were pronounced dead on arrival. Leo survived for at least another forty minutes before he too expired. Each had died as a result of a single gunshot wound to the head.

Later that tragic morning, news soon reached far and wide of the triple deaths, bringing many sightseers to the scene. A reporter from the *Pall Mall Gazette* (21 September 1893) commented thus:

*When I visited the square this morning, I found in front of the fine Presbyterian church a small crowd of gaping loafers. Elsewhere in the square the railings had leaning against them others who tried to get as much as possible out of the small sensation always to be found in gazing at the scene of a ghastly tragedy. A baker's boy paused to look on his delivery of bread, and let the hot rolls of his employers' customers go cool. A postman lingered with his bag over his shoulder on his way off duty.*

The reporter failed to mention the collection of news hounds that also 'loafed' in the square hoping for gruesome titbits. A little over forty-eight hours after the incident, the same reporter and fellow hacks were to be found at the inquest into the killings held at St Pancras Coroner's Court. Mrs Winterbottom of 24 Regent Square took the stand as a major eyewitness. She told the jury that, *she was sitting on the balcony of her residence when, having seen someone dart from the doorway of no.23, she saw Mr Garcia shot by a man, whom she had since identified as Mr Percy. The latter afterwards shot Miss Montague, and then put a revolver to his head and fired.*

Each of the bodies received one bullet only but according to witnesses four shots were heard. The minor mystery was solved when it was revealed that the first bullet fired had passed through Samuel Garcia's hat without injuring him. Following Mrs Winterbottom's testament, members of the Percy Family gave details as to Leo's state of mind leading up to the fatal occurrence. One item of great importance presented in evidence was a letter written by Leo Percy to his father and dated 11 September.[25] The correspondence was handed to John West, housekeeper of 28 Regent Square, by Leo's brother after the shooting. Mr West diligently brought the letter to the attention of the court:

*My dear Father, I have no doubt that by the time you receive this you will know all, if what I expect occurs. I can bear it no longer. The pain and humiliation is too great, so it is best ended. I determined long ago that no other one should have her and would have ended my life now but for you … I do not know that there is anything else that I have to mention. I am sorry if I give you pain, but there is nothing I can live for now. My best love to all. Your affectionate son, Percy.*

In outlining his seemingly insoluble personal predicament, Leo's letter ably described to the coroner's jury its cause and terrible solution. Given the evidence there could only be one outcome of the court's findings and, after a brief retirement, the jury found that Bessie Montague and Samuel Garcia were wilfully murdered by Leo Percy, who afterwards committed suicide whilst in a state of unsound mind. Immediately following the findings of the inquest, Samuel Garcia's body was released to relatives so that his body could be buried in accordance with Jewish rites. On Sunday, 24 September, his final resting place became the Portuguese Burial Ground, Mile End Road. Two days later, in a demonstration of public sympathy, nearly 4,000 mourners congregated in Regent Square to pay their last respects to Bessie. A ticket only funeral service was held in the aforementioned St Peter's Church, after which her body was taken to St Pancras Cemetery, East Finchley for burial. The whereabouts of the remains of Leo Percy was not disclosed.

In the annals of local crime, the Regent Square tragedy will never be hailed as sensational or even unique but its recounting allows for an insight into an incident that once caused much consternation to the local populace; the huge attendance at Bessie Montague's funeral service bears witness to this. This outpouring of grief doubtless enabled Regent Square's community to effect closure on what was then probably the darkest moment in the location's history. Alas, this was to be relatively short-lived for an equally dark episode was to occur less than twenty-five years later when a headless corpse was found early one morning in the gardens of the square (see Chapter 16)!

# CHAPTER 14

# The Camden Town Murder
# 1907

*'... and the woman's night garments, which had become her shroud,*
*were soaked with blood.'*

The arrival of the twentieth century witnessed little decline in people's propensity to commit murderous and foul deeds. Nevertheless, its predecessor had shown that, despite heinous crimes continuing, advances in legal reform and practice were being made. This progress was to carry on into the new century and, in 1907, Camden Town became the location for a particularly intriguing case that was to boast a 'judicial first'. Known as the 'Camden Town Murder', the crime attracted national interest. Its case history is still discussed today.

On the morning of 12 September 1907, 29 St Paul's Road (now Agar Grove) became the scene of the brutal murder of twenty-two-year-old blonde, Emily Elizabeth Dimmock. She shared rooms at the Camden Town address with her common-law husband Bertram Shaw, a Midland Railway dining-car attendant based at St Pancras Station. Bert worked unsociable hours serving meals on the early morning and evening trains between London and Sheffield. Meanwhile, under the name of 'Phyllis', Emily spent her time as a prostitute, a trade Bert thought she had given up when the two joined company. On 12 September, Bert arrived home from his shift around noon. Knocking at the door to his apartment, but attracting no response from Emily, he gained access using the landlady's spare key. He found his parlour to be completely ransacked with the remnants of a meal for two left on the dining table. Moving to the bedroom, the door of which he found to be locked, Bert forced his way in and was, according to the *St Pancras Gazette* (13 September 1907), 'confronted with a spectacle which was calculated to make the strongest shiver.' The newspaper account continued:

[Emily Dimmock's] *half naked body lay across the bed, and the head was slashed from the body. The poor face was lined with agony, and the still glassy, eyes gazed rigidly, but could not see. The hands were cut, and the drawn up knees lacerated. The bed and bedclothes, and the woman's night garments, which had become her shroud, were soaked with blood.*

*29 Agar Grove (formerly St Paul's Road), Camden Town, 2004.*

A distraught Bert Shaw rushed from the house and into the road looking for a policeman. Locating an officer in nearby Murray Street, the two men hurried back to the bloody crime scene. The police pathologist's examination of the body indicated Emily's death took place between 3.00 am and 6.00 am and that, in all probability, she was mercifully asleep when her throat was cut. Fortunately for the investigating detectives, the victim's movements prior to death had not been difficult to establish. For three evenings that week, as 'Phyllis' Dimmock, Emily had been entertaining a ship's cook named Robert Percival Roberts. She declined his offer of a fourth night maintaining that she had arranged a previous assignation with another client on 11 September. To prove this, Emily showed Roberts first a letter and then a postcard; both items were invitations to rendezvous that evening. The author(s) suggested two locations in which to meet, either the *Eagle* public house on the corner of Camden Road and Great (now Royal) College Street or the *Rising Sun* public house at 120 Euston Road. Both were favoured haunts of the young prostitute. These communiqués were later discovered at 29 St Paul's Road and were to become vital clues in the hunt for the killer. The letter, found partially burnt, read, 'Dear Phillis, Will you meet me at the bar of the *Eagle* at Camden Town, 8.30 tonight, Wednesday. Bert', and the postcard stated, 'Phillis Darling. If it pleases you meet me at 8.15 pm at the [*Rising Sun*]. Yours to a cinder. Alice.' In place of the words *Rising Sun* was an ably drawn

*Incriminating evidence. The publication of this postcard in newspapers led to Robert Wood's arrest for the murder of Emily 'Phyllis' Dimmock in 1907.*

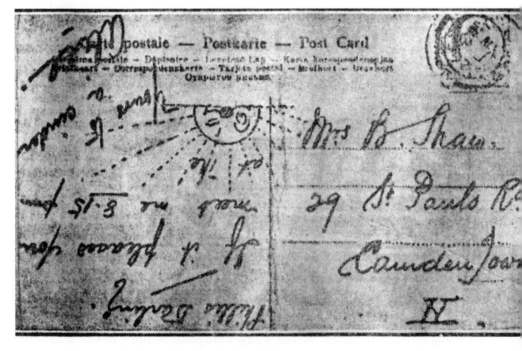

cartoon sun rising over a horizon. Both signatories were bogus but, intriguingly, the correspondence appeared to be written by the same hand. If the author of the letter was the murderer then Bert Shaw and Roberts could be discounted, as they each had watertight alibis for the night in question. So who could be the mysterious correspondent? For help, the police turned to the newspapers.

When the postcard was printed in the *News of the World*, its handwriting and pictorial doodling were recognised by artists' model and local prostitute, Ruby Young. She knew it to be the work of an ex-boyfriend, the flamboyantly named Robert William Thomas George Cavers Wood. Despite the chance of gaining £100 reward, Ruby did not initially inform the police of her discovery and she even concocted an alibi for the twenty-eight-year-old Wood. But, feeling guilty of withholding such vital information, Ruby later mentioned the handwriting to a friend who then passed the information on. Eventually, the authorities picked up the trail. Described in appearance as being 'shabby genteel', Wood was a graphic designer who, from his lodgings he shared with his father and half-brother at 12 Frederick Street, King's Cross, also made extra money as an amateur artist. After discussing picture postcards with 'Phyllis', when he met her for the first time at the *Rising Sun* on 6 September, Wood sent her an example of his artwork on the aforementioned postcard. He signed the card 'Alice' in order to allay any suspicions that Bert Shaw may have should he find it at home. Meanwhile, and in keeping with the invitation found in the related letter, witnesses testified that they saw Robert Wood in the company of 'Phyllis' at the *Eagle* as late as 11 pm on 11 September, only hours before her death. Even more damning was the allegation that Wood was spotted leaving 29 St Paul's Road at 4.40 am on the morning of the murder by unemployed carman, Robert McGowan, on his way to a potential job. The net of evidence against Wood was now closing in and his arrest seemed imminent. Indeed, on 7 October, and under the watchful eye of Detective Inspector Arthur Neill and his men, Ruby arranged to meet Wood in Gray's Inn Road. As soon as the couple greeted each other, Neill interrupted the meeting and took the artist into custody for questioning. Before being led off, Wood turned to his 'ex' and dramatically said, 'Good-bye, dear, don't worry. I have to go with these gentlemen; if England wants me, she must have me: don't cry, but be true.' To which Ruby replied, 'Leave that to me.' At Clerkenwell Police Court, Robert Wood was charged with Emily's murder. Upon interrogation, he stuck to the alibi he had earlier fabricated with Ruby Young but little did Wood know that she had not remained true!

Kings Cross Police Station & Clerkenwell
Police Court. W. C.

*Clerkenwell Police Court (left), c.1906, where Robert Wood was formally charged with the murder of Emily Dimmock.*

By late October, and with the artist now on remand for the killing, the jury at St Pancras Coroner's Court had confirmed a verdict of wilful murder. The date of 12 December 1907 was subsequently set for Wood's trial at the Central Criminal Court, Old Bailey. Although evidence against him was circumstantial, it appeared strong enough for a conviction but the prosecution failed to anticipate the skill and guile of his defence barrister, Mr (later Sir) Edward Marshall-Hall. During the six-day trial, the public warmed to Wood. Inexplicably, the masses even took offence at Ruby's eleventh hour betrayal. Further empathy was felt towards the artist when he stepped into the witness-box to give evidence. Under Marshall-Hall's adroit questioning, and despite appearing a little over confident, with a tendency to pose, Wood made a good impression in court. Following his performance in the dock, and for the remainder of the trial, the prisoner became somewhat detached from the proceedings, preferring instead to sketch. Meanwhile, his resourceful barrister successfully cast doubt on prosecution evidence.

*The trial of Robert Wood (top left) for the Camden Town Murder makes headline news.*

He established that his client had no motive for murder, especially as Wood had only met Emily (as 'Phyllis') for the first time less than a week before her death. As they were undated, Marshall-Hall even dismissed the seemingly incriminating correspondence as whimsy, arguing that they did not represent direct invitations for his client to meet with

Dimmock. It was conceded that the artist did spend the evening of 11 September at the *Eagle* with 'Phyllis' but left her at 11.00 pm and returned home to Frederick Street. Serious doubt was also cast upon the testament of the carman who thought he saw Wood leaving 29 St Paul's Road on the morning of the murder. He had only seen the back of the suspect and could not positively identify the person, despite earlier stating that he recognised Wood's style of walking as being similar to that of the man seen leaving the scene of the crime.

During his summation on 18 December, Mr Justice Grantham was clearly struck by the persuasive character of the prisoner and warned the jury against the dangers of a conviction based purely on circumstantial evidence. No sooner had the jury retired to consider a verdict that they returned twenty minutes later to declare Robert Wood not guilty of murder. In what appeared to be certain conviction at the commencement of the trial became a triumphant and popular acquittal. From inside the court, as well as from the thousands waiting expectantly outside, jubilant cheers greeted the verdict. And more significantly, Wood became the first defendant in a murder trial to be acquitted after giving evidence at his own trial. After the celebrations subsided, the ill fated Ruby Young left the court building disguised as a charwoman to avoid the mob's wrath, whereas the defendant and his family went on to enjoy a celebratory meal.

Emily Dimmock was buried on 17 September 1907 at St Pancras Cemetery, East Finchley, unaware of the role she was to later play in criminal lore. Apart from the sensational trial of Robert Wood, another, more permanent reminder of the young prostitute, and events surrounding her death, was to be created a year later by eminent artist, Walter Sickert, himself a Camden Town resident. Sickert's *The Camden Town Murder Series* featured two paintings, each depicting a naked woman lying on a bed accompanied by a fully clothed man positioned by her side. The first of these, *What shall we do for the rent?* (1908), was followed with *L'affaire de Camden Town* (1909). Despite the latter's name, neither work was a re-creation of the murder but, by naming the series after 'The Camden Town Murder', Sickert took advantage of the publicity such a title would attract. It has been suggested that Wood, an acquaintance of Sickert, even modelled for the paintings' male character. In a recent and controversial interpretation of these portrayals of Camden Town low-life, American crime novelist and former mortuary assistant Patricia Cornwell alleges that Walter Sickert was none other than 'Jack the Ripper'. Presenting her theory in 2001, and prompted by the murder of Emily Dimmock, she believes that the paintings share a similarity with the autopsy photographs taken of the

Whitechapel murderer's victims in 1888. Cornwell spent £2 million buying Sickert paintings and other personal artefacts in a bid to prove her theory. Needless to say, her allegations have met with derision from both the art world and criminologists.

What remains fact, however, is that Emily's killer remained at large. The only ever likely candidate was Robert Wood but with help from an outstanding defence barrister, an unaccountably sympathetic public, and a somewhat biased judge, the evidence against the young artist was simply not enough to convict. The verdict of not guilty is still somewhat questionable but, if the jury and public were convinced as to his innocence in the affair, who was the real killer? Alas, the answer to this is destined to remain as much a mystery as that which surrounds the true identity of 'Jack the Ripper' himself!

# CHAPTER 15

# The Crime of the Century: The Infamous Case of Dr Crippen
## 1910

*Discovered buried ... was ... a headless, 'filleted' corpse wrapped parcel-like in a piece of pyjama jacket.*

One of the most infamous names ever to have been convicted for murder in Britain is that of Dr Hawley Harvey Crippen. Almost a century after his trial and execution at the age of forty-eight years, his sinister sounding moniker still evokes an eerie sensation of malevolence. Only three years after the brutal slaying of Emily Dimmock (see Chapter 14), Camden Town witnessed American-born Crippen play the central role in a notoriously grisly murder that similarly was to not only shock Edwardian society but also introduce yet more 'criminological firsts'.

Born in Coldwater, Michigan, in 1862, Dr Crippen was not a qualified doctor but had acquired diplomas in medicine and pharmacology. He and his Polish-German second wife, Cora Turner (formerly Kunigunde Mackamotzki), whom he married in 1892, came to England in 1900. The American's qualifications were not sufficient for him to practice as a doctor in Britain, so instead he peddled patent medicines for Munyon's Remedies. Meanwhile, his wife aspired to a life in music-hall under the stage name of 'Belle Elmore'. Theirs was a loveless and often quarrelsome marriage. Crippen was a timid and well liked, bespectacled man, whereas his wife was domineering and aggressive, frequently humiliating him in public. They lived in a series of addresses in St Pancras and Holborn and, in

*Dr Hawley Harvey Crippen, perpetrator of what was described in 1910 as the 'crime of the century'.*

1905, the Crippens moved to 39 Hilldrop Crescent. Although the address lay near Holloway, it was regularly reported as being in Camden Town. By 1907, Crippen had employed a secretary, Ethel Le Neve, to work with him at his firm's New Oxford Street office. It was not long until employer and secretary began an 'intrigue', with the two often meeting in seedy hotels in Argyle Square, King's Cross. Their affair grew in commitment. Ethel had even suffered a miscarriage but, with the impossible and increasingly abusive Cora ever present, their relationship could not blossom. Crippen and his mistress doubtless prayed daily for his wife to vanish and, early in 1910, the lovers' godly appeals were seemingly answered, for Cora Crippen suddenly disappeared. There was, alas, no divine intervention. Dr Crippen had

*Cora Crippen as music-hall singer 'Belle Elmore', now infamously immortalised as the wife and victim of Dr Crippen.*

simply answered his own prayers, deliberately ensuring that his wife was never to come between Ethel and himself again! On 12 March, a little over two months after Cora's disappearance, Ms Le Neve left her lodgings at 80 Constantine Road, Hampstead, and moved into the Hilldrop Crescent residence.

Suspicious of their friend's departure, Crippen told his wife's music-hall colleagues that she had returned to America where, after an unexpected illness, she had unfortunately died. He even placed her obituary in the *Era*, a show business newspaper. Other than her husband, the last time anyone had seen Cora alive was on the evening of 31 January 1910 at Hilldrop Crescent when the Crippens had entertained some friends. Cora's many associates still remained unconvinced by Crippen's story, especially when Ethel was sighted wearing his wife's jewellery and furs. So, they decided to confront the doctor. Crippen was asked if he knew where his wife had died, to which he replied, 'some little town near San Francisco, with a Spanish name

*The scene of the crime: 39 Hilldrop Crescent, July 1910.*

I think.' Sceptical of his answer, their concerns were reported to Scotland Yard on 30 June. After considering the circumstances surrounding the music-hall performer's abrupt departure, Chief Inspector Walter Dew decided that Crippen should be investigated and, on 8 July, he and Sergeant Mitchell visited Hilldrop Crescent. Crippen was clearly shaken by the arrival of the police and began to change his story. The doctor admitted to Dew that the story about his wife's illness and subsequent death were untrue and that, as far as he knew, she was still very much alive. He went on to explain that Cora had eloped with a lover, Bruce Miller, and he (Crippen) had been too humiliated publicly to admit this and so had fabricated a story about her death. This, in part, was true. His wife had previously taken lovers and one, a German student, even lodged with them at Hilldrop Crescent. Dew and Mitchell searched the house but found nothing suspicious. The Chief Inspector also accepted Crippen's explanation about Cora's disappearance but informed him that he would return the next day to finish off the investigation. In the meantime, scared at what the police might uncover, the doctor panicked and took immediate flight with his companion.

The couple's hasty departure led to several searches of the residence and eventually the police found what they were looking for, namely the remains of Cora Crippen otherwise 'Belle Elmore'. Discovered buried in lime under the coal cellar floor of 39 Hilldrop Crescent was what could only be described a headless, 'filleted' corpse wrapped parcel-like in a piece of pyjama jacket. Cora's head, limbs and bones were missing, never to be found. In his first major case, famous British pathologist Bernard Spilsbury established that, from scar tissue and a fringe of hair, the torso definitely belonged to Mrs Crippen. The remains also contained traces of the poison hyoscin hydrobromide; Crippen was found to have purchased five grains of hyoscin in January 1910. This was apparently the first time that this somewhat obscure toxin had been used for murderous purposes. It was estimated that the murder took place on or around Tuesday, 1 February that year. This tied in neatly with her last known sighting. Mercifully, Cora's body had been mutilated after death but exactly when the poison was administered and where and how her dissection took place were never determined. This pathological evidence was to prove crucial in the later conviction of the doctor. On 16 July, Dew obtained a worldwide warrant for the arrest of Crippen and Le Neve and, with their descriptions in circulation, the police began a major hunt for the fugitives.

The two had, in fact, made their way to the continent. In Antwerp, they boarded the SS *Montrose* bound for Montreal, Canada. The steamship's eagle-eyed skipper, Captain Henry Kendall, became suspicious of the two passengers after he had read about the crime. He also recognised Crippen's photograph from a newspaper report. The couple were masquerading as Mr John and Master Robinson, father

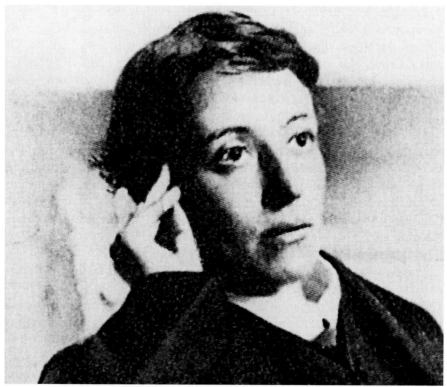

*Ethel Le Neve in disguise as Master Robinson whilst on the run with her lover, Dr Crippen.*

and son, with Ethel playing the latter role. On 22 July, the Captain telegraphed his now historic marconigram from the *Montrose* to authorities ashore. Fortunately, the ship was one of only a few to be equipped with new radio technology. His message read:

> *Have strong suspicion that Crippen London Cellar murderer and accomplice are amongst saloon passengers. Moustache shaved off, growing a beard. Accomplice dressed as a boy, voice, manner and build undoubtedly a girl.*

This was the first ever use of radiotelegraphy for police purposes. As a result, Chief Inspector Dew was able to take immediate passage on a faster vessel, the SS *Laurentic*, and catch up with the *Montrose* in Canadian waters before it reached its destination. On 31 July, he boarded Captain Kendall's ship at Father's Point and duly arrested Crippen and Le Neve. The high seas drama caused a sensation in the press and, with daily coverage of events on board, the murder was soon hailed as 'the crime of the century'.

Crippen and Ethel Le Neve were tried separately before Lord Alverstone, Lord Chief Justice of England, at the Central Criminal Court. Such was the demand to attend Crippen's trial that over 4,000 applications were received requesting seats. In their eagerness to cover every minutiae of the case, the press even managed to illegally sneak cameras into court to record the event for their detail hungry readers. Proceedings began on 18 October with the prisoner entering a plea of not guilty. The *John Bull* weekly newspaper offered to pay Crippen's legal fees and hired Arthur Newton to defend him; the barrister was later to become the prison librarian at Pentonville Prison. The prosecution, on the other hand, was relentless in its pursuit of a conviction, and Spilsbury's findings were to prove pivotal to its success. The trial concluded on 22 October with the jury taking just thirty minutes to return a unanimous verdict of guilty. Crippen was heard to say, 'I still protest my innocence', after which Lord Alverstone sentenced the murderer to the obligatory death by hanging. Better fortune befell Ethel Le Neve at her trial commencing Tuesday, 25 October. She was charged only with being an accessory after the fact to the murder. Deciding not to give evidence in the witness box, Crippen's mistress was found not guilty and acquitted. She left for Canada only to return to England where she married and raised a family in relative anonymity. Meanwhile, Crippen paid the ultimate price for his short spell of happiness with her. His love for Ethel remained true to the end and was demonstrated when he was permitted to keep her letters and photo on his person during and after his execution. Despite a petition containing over 15,000 signatures requesting that Crippen's execution be suspended, he was hanged at Pentonville Prison at 9 am on Wednesday, 23 November 1910. Afterwards, a large crowd congregated outside the prison gates to witness the posting of the execution notice. An unmarked grave within the precincts of Pentonville became his final resting place.

It has since emerged that crucial evidence was seemingly withheld from Crippen's defence team.[26] Some ninety years after the trial, letters have surfaced that were apparently written, signed and posted by Cora Crippen from Chicago after her husband's conviction. One letter, dated 25 October 1910 and addressed to the Governor of Pentonville Prison, pleads for her husband to be spared the death penalty. Another was passed to the then Home Secretary, Winston Churchill. This too was filed and ignored and its contents never divulged. It was also revealed that Cora Crippen 'posthumously' withdrew money from her bank account but again this lead was never followed up. Furthermore, it has been claimed that supposed payments to witnesses were made for false

*Margaret Bondfield House now occupies the site of Crippen's former address at 39 Hilldrop Crescent.*

testimony against Crippen. For example, Bruce Miller, a former lover of Cora's, was paid $450 for his allegedly erroneous statement. Was Dr Crippen therefore a victim of a gross miscarriage of justice? But, if innocent, why then did he take flight? And, if not Cora's, whose remains were buried in the cellar? In spite of the evidential revelations, which only serve to add further mystery to an already incredible story of forbidden love, murder and escape, the general opinion remains that the hen-pecked Crippen did kill his wife so that he could devote himself entirely to Ethel. Had his nerve held, when initially interviewed by Chief Inspector Dew, he and his mistress may have lived a long and loving life. Instead, his panic led to the couple's prompt capture by an effective combination of police tactics, media publicity, the use of recent advances in telecommunications and, perhaps still the most valuable of all detection aids, public intervention.

Today, Dr Crippen's house at 39 Hilldrop Crescent no longer exists. Following damage caused by bombing during the Second World War, it and adjoining buildings were demolished and replaced with Margaret Bondfield House, a block of flats. Nonetheless, in spite of number 39's eradication, the location will always be remembered for one its former residents and one of Britain's 'great' criminals, namely Dr Hawley Harvey Crippen, and his involvement in what then was claimed to be 'the crime of the century'.

# CHAPTER 16

# *L'Affaire Diabolique de Charlotte Street:* The 'butchering' of Emilienne Gerard
# 1917

*... decapitation and amputation ... were quite skilfully performed ...*

*On Friday morning* [2 November 1917] *the mutilated body of a woman, wrapped in a sheet of sacking, was found lying just inside the railing of the garden at Gray's Inn road. The head and hands had been removed and were missing: the legs, severed at the knees, were found in a separate parcel a few feet farther inside the railings; on the trunk was a piece of brown paper, on which was scribbled the words 'Blodie Belgim'; and the body was naked except for a vest and a chemise ornamented with lace and ribbon.*

Thus reported the *St Pancras Gazette* (9 November 1917), introducing a story of which even today's sensation seeking tabloid press would be envious. The fact that Britain then was still locked in bitter confrontation with Germany did not seemingly deter some on the home front from satisfying their own bloodlust. The garden located in Regent Square, St Pancras, had once again become the backdrop of yet another foul deed (see Chapter 13). This time, it was local resident Thomas George Henry, a packer in a store on his way to work, who first made the grim discovery at 8.30 am on the day in question. He first noticed the main bundle containing the torso, which he initially thought to be half a sheep, lying about four feet west of the garden's south gate adjacent to Compton Street (now Tavistock Place). With the appropriate authorities alerted, evidence unearthed at the scene was to prove crucial in solving the mystery behind a death in what were clearly suspicious circumstances.

Dr John Gabe, a police surgeon from nearby Mecklenburgh Square, estimated that the victim had been dead at least twenty-four hours and the lack of fresh blood about the remains indicated that death occurred elsewhere. He further deduced that decapitation and amputation of the lower legs and hands were quite skilfully performed by someone possessing knowledge of anatomy, a butcher perhaps? The outer covering housing the torso was a brown paper meat sack containing the stencilled words 'La Plate Cold Storage, Argentina'. This had the crudely written 'Blodie Belgim' also scrawled upon it. Moreover, the inner sacking in which the remains were wrapped was to provide investigating officer Chief Inspector Wensley and his colleagues with an exceptional clue. A laundry mark, 'II H', was found embroidered on one of its corners. Cleverly, the mark was traced to 50 Munster Square, a property located to the west of Euston Station, in the Regent's Park area of St Pancras. One of its tenants was thirty-two-year-old French woman, Emilienne Gerard. Furthermore, it was discovered that she had been missing since 31 October, a date when the area experienced a heavy enemy air raid. A cursory search of Mme Gerard's rooms produced more clues. An IOU note for £50 signed by a certain Louis Marie Joseph Voisin and a framed photograph of him was found amongst her possessions.

*Madame Emilienne Gerard who, after fleeing her Regent's Park home to escape a German air raid, was later brutally murdered at the hands of her lover and his 'other' lover. Portrait drawn by Rachel Dilworth from a contemporary press illustration.*

Voisin was traced to 101 Charlotte Street, a somewhat squalid residence situated near Fitzroy Square and only ten minutes walk from Munster Square. A fifty-year-old Frenchman and butcher by trade but then working as a stableman, Voisin was a stout, powerfully built moustached man who shared his Fitzrovia address with French widow, Berthe Roche. Through an interpreter, Chief Inspector Wensley questioned the Gallic couple about the disappearance of Mme Gerard at Bow Street Police Station. The butcher admitted that he knew the missing woman and had enjoyed an 'intimate' relationship with her after they had first met the previous year. Voisin explained that he had last seen Mme Gerard on 31 October just prior to her departure for France, where she was to visit her husband, Paul Gerard, a soldier serving in the 79th French Infantry Regiment. The butcher claimed that she asked him to feed her pet cat during her absence abroad. Meanwhile, thirty-eight-year-old Roche, who had lost her soldier husband early in the war, denied that she even knew Voisin's paramour. Interrogation continued into the following day during which the Frenchman was invited to write out the phrase

*Ordnance Survey map of 1914. Louis Voisin's house at 101 Charlotte Street was the first building to the left of Bedford Passage (looking towards Howland Street).*

'Bloody Belgium'. This he did willingly and, having reproduced the words five times, on each occasion he incorrectly spelt the phrase using the exact mis-spelling found inscribed on the brown paper sacking containing the victim's torso. Voisin's facsimiles also closely matched

*'Le duo diabolique', Berthe Roche and Louis Voisin. Portraits drawn by Rachel Dilworth from a contemporary press illustration.*

the original in style of handwriting. The case was beginning to take shape and more grisly evidence was gathered when Wensley and his men decided to re-visit 101 Charlotte Street.

Louis Voisin's kitchen and adjoining floors, walls and ceilings were found to be splashed with blood; the Frenchman claimed this was by-product from a recently slaughtered animal. Furthermore, a search of the building's cellar by Detective Sergeant Collins resulted in the discovery of a female human head and hands hidden in a barrel of sawdust. These remains were identified as belonging to Emilienne Gerard. This discovery alone was enough for the police to charge Voisin and Roche with the wilful murder of their compatriot. *The Times* (17 January 1918) reported that when the charge was interpreted to them Roche turned to Voisin in a rage and, addressing him by a French term of abuse, but of a very definite meaning, said, 'You have deceived me.' Voisin said, 'It is unfortunate.' He also gallantly added, 'Mme Roche is not concerned with the crime at all.' In the meantime, Paul Gerard had arrived in London on special leave to identify Emilienne's 're-assembled' body and attend the inquest into her death. This done, he then proceeded with her burial at St Pancras Cemetery, East Finchley, on 13 November.

To help with forensic evidence, the police recruited pathologist Bernard Spilsbury, whose expert work on the earlier Crippen case (see

Chapter 15) proved crucial in securing a conviction. Assisted by Dr Gabe, the forensic expert performed a post-mortem examination upon the remains of Mme Gerard. Concentrating on the poor woman's decapitated and severely battered head, the post-mortem showed that it contained many fractures, bruises and lacerations, a number of which exposed bone. Spilsbury decided that these injuries occurred before death and could not have been accidental. They were caused as a result of 'several blows with a blunt instrument while she was lying on the ground, and that the weapon must have scattered blood as it rose and fell.' The latter observation could account for the sprays of blood found in Voisin's kitchen. He thought that death occurred at least thirty minutes or more after the attack began but its severity would have caused immediate unconsciousness. The expert concluded that death was due to shock and loss of blood following the injuries to the head and that 'there were signs of blood on the heart which indicated asphyxia.'

*Paul Gerard, the husband of the victim. Gerard left the horrors of 'the front' only to be even more horrified by his wife's death in London. He later broke down as he identified her body at St Pancras Mortuary. Portrait drawn by Rachel Dilworth from a contemporary press illustration.*

Given the evidence so far collected, the investigators reconstructed what they believed to be the final hours of Mme Gerard. Events apparently began on Wednesday, 31 October. During the morning, Mme Gerard had been in the company of a lady friend, Marguerite, who was returning to France that day. Eyewitness John Brisse, a proprietor of a café in Whitfield Street who knew Mme Gerard and who had seen her that morning, noticed that she was in lively spirits and appeared in good health. Little then was known of her exact movements until much later that evening, when an air-raid of German Gotha bombers threatened the safety of all those residing in the capital. It was surmised that, around 11 pm, Emilienne had sought shelter from the raid first at a local underground station, possibly Warren Street, and then at her lover's Charlotte Street house. Arriving unexpectedly, she no doubt startled Berthe Roche. Previously, Mme Gerard was unaware of the butcher's live-in partner and, in a later statement, Roche claimed that she too had never met Emilienne until that night. All fear of the raid was forgotten as the two Frenchwomen entered into a violent argument regarding the 'ménage a trois'. In a jealous rage, Roche flew at Mme Gerard and attacked her with a blunt instrument, possibly a poker, causing widespread cranial damage. Bernard Spilsbury theorised that it was she that attacked the victim first and not Voisin, as the wounds would have been even more profound had the more powerful hand of the Frenchman wielded the weapon. At this point Voisin joined in and, in an attempt to silence the victim's screams, he smothered her with a towel whilst Roche continue to strike. This corroborated Spilsbury's finding that attempted strangulation had occurred, plus a bloodied towel was found at the scene containing one of Mme Gerard's earrings that had snagged in the attack.

After the murder, and exercising his butchering skills, Voisin dismembered the body. He then took the remains to 50 Munster Square where he smeared blood around the kitchen to suggest the foul deed had occurred at Mme Gerard's rooms; bloodstains were found at the address by Spilsbury in a later forensic search. The Frenchman told the landlord of the Regent's Park residence that he was expecting a delivery of a sack of potatoes. This ruse was one of a number to confuse potential investigations; the 'Blodie Belgi[a]m' note on the victim's torso and animal blood used to camouflage human blood found in the Charlotte Street kitchen were others. Further confusion as to events was witnessed at the French couple's trial, which commenced on 16 January 1918 before Mr Justice Darling at the Central Criminal Court. Both defendants vehemently protested their innocence and pleaded not guilty to the charge of wilful murder. The jury heard a statement made previously to Chief Inspector Wensley by Voisin on how he went to Mme Gerard's rooms on 1 November to find the floor and carpet awash with blood and her severed head and hands were lying on the kitchen table. He added,

> I thought a trap had been laid for me … I commenced to clean the place … and later fetched them [the head and hands] away. I cannot see why I should do such a thing to her. I knew Mme Gerard was keeping bad company, taking people to her flat. I knew she had taken somebody there that night.

This statement conflicted wildly to an earlier assertion that the butcher thought Emilienne had travelled to France to see her husband. The court then heard Bernard Spilsbury give forensic evidence and, to further explain his post-mortem conclusions, both pathologist and jury visited 101 Charlotte Street on day two of the trial. Other witnesses for the prosecution were called, including Police Constable Bendall who, at the earlier pre-trial hearing at Marlborough Street Police Court, had stated that he saw Voisin returning from the direction of King's Cross in a dog cart less than a hour before the remains were discovered in Regent Square.

The general consensus of opinion was that jealousy and not, as some believed, money was the motive for murder; the £50 debt owed by Voisin now seemed incidental. Three days after the trial opened the jury listened intently to Justice Darling's summing up in which he highlighted the discrepancies in statements made by the Frenchman, as well as drawing attention to the damning evidence of human remains and blood discovered at 101 Charlotte Street. After what the defence later believed to a biased summation against Voisin, the jury returned a verdict of guilty in just fifteen minutes. To this finding, the prisoner announced, 'I have to say that I am innocent.' Then, the sentence of death was passed by the judge in both French and English. Charges of murder against Berthe Roche were dismissed but an indictment of being an accessory after the fact to murder was brought against her. In a separate trial commencing on 27 February, she was found guilty and sentenced to seven years penal servitude. Roche did not complete her incarceration and, in a little over a year after her trial, she became insane and died in a mental asylum on 22 March 1919. Meanwhile, Voisin's defence team appealed against his conviction on the grounds of incorrect police procedures prior to his arrest; he had not been under arrest at the time he gave examples of his handwriting and therefore the evidence was inadmissible. The team also believed that the judge had misdirected the trial jury. Needless to say, the appeal failed and Voisin was hanged on 2 March 1918 at Pentonville Prison by Chief Executioner John Ellis.

No trace remains today of 101 Charlotte Street or 50 Munster Square, both were swept away as a result of post-Second World War redevelopment. The gardens of Regent Square do still exist and serve as a reminder of a grisly crime of jealously that, as in 1893, ultimately claimed three lives. What often remains untold is the story of those left behind, largely forgotten by events beyond their control. In this case, Paul Gerard. What became of him in the years following his wife's murder is unknown but it can only be hoped that he was able to pick up the pieces of his shattered life and begin life anew in the brave new world that the conclusion of World War One claimed to offer.

# CHAPTER 17

# The Burning Shed Mystery: The Plight of Samuel Furnace
# 1933

*... the public was captivated by the nationwide manhunt ...*

For the residents of Camden Town, 1933 began, as all years do, with the hope of a happy and prosperous new year ahead. These sentiments were undoubtedly abandoned when, in early January, the area experienced an extraordinary murder.

Superintendent Cornish and his police colleagues were alerted to an incident that had taken place in Hawley Crescent, a busy thoroughfare located at the north end of Camden High Street. Forty-two-year-old builder and decorator Samuel James Furnace of Crogsland Road, Chalk Farm, had been found burned to death in his office, a shed at the rear of 30 Hawley Crescent belonging to John Wynne; a restaurant now occupies the site. At around 8 pm on Tuesday, 3 January 1933, Mr

*In 2004, this fashionable eatery in Hawley Crescent, Camden Town, occupies of the site of the 'burning shed', the scene of Walter Spatchett's murder in 1933.*

Wynne noticed that the property he rented to Furnace was ablaze and so summoned the fire brigade. Once the fire had been extinguished, the charred body of a man sitting on a high stool in front of the remains of a desk was discovered in the burnt out ruins of the shed. The victim was initially identified as being Samuel Furnace and, to further confirm this, a suicide note signed by the builder was found in an adjacent tool shed that had escaped the flames. It read, 'Good-bye to all – no work, no money.' Despite giving priority to the payment of £28 for an insurance premium only a month earlier, that would benefit his wife and three children in the event of his death, it was true that he was experiencing moderate financial difficulties. He was overdrawn at the bank, he owed £59 to various tradesmen in Kentish Town and his rent and rates were in arrears. And so it seemed, to Furnace, that suicide was an effective way of solving his monetary troubles.

Enter celebrated St Pancras Coroner William Bentley Purchase into the investigation. Immediately becoming suspicious of both the circumstances surrounding the death and the identity of the body, he decided to examine Furnace's corpse himself. Fortunately, fragments of clothing had survived the blaze and the victim's teeth remained quite unharmed by the fire. With the help of pathologist Dr John Taylor, Bentley Purchase discovered that the victim had been shot in the right side of the back and was dead before being set alight. The post-mortem also revealed that his teeth belonged to a man younger than Furnace. Next, a search of the charred clothes on the body revealed a post office savings book bearing the name Walter Spatchett, a twenty-four-year-old local rent collector of Dartmouth Park Road. At the Coroner's invitation, Spatchett's doctor, Leo Clarke, was present at the post-mortem and recalled that, just like the victim's teeth, his patient's outer incisor protruded outwards with a

*Samuel Furnace. His attempted fake suicide ultimately led to real suicide.*

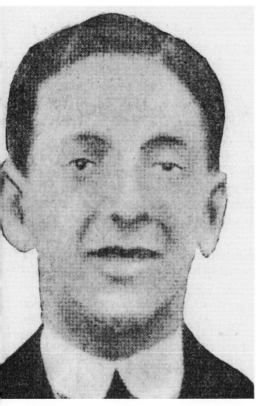

*Walter Spatchett, the 'burning shed' victim.*

marked 'tilt'. Walter Spatchett's father backed up this evidence by positively identifying personal effects and the remains of clothing found on his son's body. With the true identity of the burnt body now established, the investigation turned into one of murder and the police now concentrated on the search for Samuel Furnace. As Cornish organised resources, the Spatchett family buried Walter on 11 January at Highgate Cemetery following a simple and dignified service.

It transpired that Furnace and Spatchett were well acquainted. The builder had previously worked for the same company of house agents that employed Spatchett and, on occasion, he would still undertake contract work for them. Furnace was described as being a plump, cheerful and open handed man and his young friend was an amiable man and an enthusiastic sportsman. The pair they would often meet socially to play billiards. On the day before the fire, Walter Spatchett had collected approximately £36 in rent payments. He should have arrived back at the office of his employers, T B Westacott and Son of 74 Camden Road, at around 5.30 pm. However, when he failed to appear for work the next morning, a messenger was sent to his home only to find that Spatchett had disappeared.

Meanwhile, the public was captivated by the nationwide manhunt for Furnace now in full swing. He was last seen in London on 5 January and, a week after the fire, the builder had still evaded capture. So, a further description of the near six foot tall, fair haired fugitive was broadcast:

*Furnace may now be wearing a very light coloured trench coat, with a brown and red check lining, double breasted, with three buttons and belt with sliding buckle, vent at the back and edged with brown leatherette binding.*

With his photograph displayed in newspapers and cinemas, sightings of the elusive builder had been reported throughout England. In fact, it was in Southend that Furnace was to give himself away, thus enabling Superintendent Cornish to finally 'get his man'. The builder made the mistake of writing to his brother-in-law, Charles Tuckfield, requesting that he bring some clothes to a location in the Essex resort. Date stamped 14 January 1933, Tuckfield handed the letter into Kentish Town Police Station. Addressed 'Dear Charlie' and signed 'H Farmer', presumably to avoid detection, he explained that he was in hiding near Southend Station, pretending to have influenza. Furnace added, 'I don't think I have slept one hour since the accident happened. I will tell you all about it when I see you.' On 15 January, only a day after the correspondence was posted, Cornish persuaded Tuckfield to carry out his brother-in-law's request whilst being shadowed by detectives. The trail led to a lodging house at 11 Whitegate Road, Southend, where Furnace signalled his presence to his relative by placing a sheet of paper in the front window displaying the letters 'SAM'. The two brothers-in-law conversed inside for two hours during which time Furnace protested that Spatchett had been shot by accident. Sometime later, Cornish and his detectives entered the premises and arrested Furnace. On being told that 'his number was up', Samuel Furnace offered no resistance. He even told the police where he disposed of the Webley revolver used to 'accidentally' kill Spatchett and, nearing Kentish Town Police Station, he indicated a spot in the Regent's Canal near Camden Street Bridge where he threw the weapon. It was recovered by police two days later.

In custody, and after being relieved of £29 in cash and two letters, Furnace confessed to the killing but maintained that the gun had gone off by mistake. In his statement he told of how Spatchett had come to his office to talk about some building work and, in conversation, he mentioned to his friend that he had a loaded revolver in his desk. He handed the gun to Spatchett who, having cocked it, became nervous and handed it back so that it could be made safe. At approximately 5.30 pm, as the young man left the office, Furnace explained that 'the gun went off and shot him. He fell to the ground moaning. I realised my position and lost my head. I went out. When I got back there, I found him dead … Next morning, about 7.15, I dragged him into the office.' Furnace then described how he concocted the idea of burning the body and making out that it was his own. In faking his own suicide, he would use it as an opportunity to escape his financial predicament. After further explaining how he used paint and oil as an accelerant, Furnace signed the confession and was placed in a cell. With a confession secured and post-mortem evidence conclusive, Furnace's conviction would be a mere formality but, in an ironic twist of fate, his bogus suicide would in fact become reality!

Complaining of a cold cell, Furnace was given both his overcoat and his new trench coat to wear. He had been searched twice previously and police had no reason to believe he would harm himself and, besides, he was under constant surveillance. It was at dawn the next morning that panic was to break out when Constable Partridge called out to Sergeant Bunthorpe, the station officer, 'Quick! He's drinking something from a bottle!' Furnace had swallowed hydrochloric acid from a small bottle he had secreted in the lining of his overcoat that had been overlooked in the earlier searches. Sergeant Bunthorpe forced Furnace's now clenched teeth open so that he could force him to drink milk and water to help counter the fearsome effects of the acid. In writhing agony, the prisoner was immediately rushed to St Pancras Infirmary. With his face turning deep purple in colour and his mouth and lips stained brown, he lingered on the threshold of death for twenty-four hours but finally succumbed to the fatal potion early on Tuesday, 17 January. The inquest into his death was held at St Pancras Coroner's Court the following day. Concluding a full hearing under the watchful eye of Coroner William Bentley Purchase, the jury returned a verdict of suicide after just two minutes of deliberation. On Friday, 20 January, the inquest into the death of Walter Spatchett was itself concluded and, after retiring for four minutes, the jury decided upon a verdict of murder. At this, Bentley Purchase concluded:

*I shall say that Walter Spatchett died on January 2, that the cause of his death was a bullet wound in his chest caused by the firing of a pistol by Samuel James Furnace, and that Furnace murdered Walter Spatchett.*

Following the inquests, the Britannic Assurance Company refused Mrs Alice Furnace's claim upon her late husband's insurance. As his death was deliberate, this caused the policy to become null and void. Spatchett's life was also insured with the Britannic and, owing to the nature of his death, a claim by his family was paid in full. In sympathy with Furnace's widow, the company did offer her a compensatory grant. And lastly, after legal argument at Marylebone Police Court, the whole sorry affair was officially closed when Mrs Furnace was granted the £29 found in her husband's possession following arrest. Spatchett's employers argued that the amount was part of the rent collected by the murdered worker. The magistrate decided otherwise and awarded the amount to the poor widow.

Debate surrounding the murder continued long after conclusion of the legal processes and focused on motive and whether Furnace had told the truth about the way Spatchett had died. The builder's story did indeed contain many inconsistencies. If supposing, albeit extremely unlikely, that his friend's death was a horrible accident why then didn't Furnace call for immediate help? His reason for burning the body was equally questionable; the execution of the fake suicide was extremely inept and ill conceived. Furnace's declaration that Spatchett visited his office to discuss work on the fateful day was also flawed. In reality, the young rent collector had no authority to employ workers on Westacott's behalf. And, why keep a loaded revolver unless it was intended for use? Ultimately, if Furnace's story was true why would he have taken his own life if he believed his account of events to be accurate? Motive for the murder was in all probability robbery but, as Bentley Purchase told the jury at Spatchett's inquest, 'there need not necessarily be any motive', but warned, 'very often motive explains why a murder took place, but very often murder can take place without a motive.'[27] An appropriate epitaph for what was an extraordinary case.

CHAPTER 18

# Make Do and Murder: Foul Deeds During Wartime

# 1941–44

*... she had been strangled with her own cami-knickers.*

Life on the home front for the civilian population of north-west London during the Second World War was difficult at the best of times but most 'did their bit' in order to live a near normal existence. Yet, for a small minority, the war represented a time when normality and morality could be cast aside, often with tragic consequences. Between 1938 and 1945, the prison population in Britain actually increased by fifty per cent.[28] As well as crimes of greed and profiteering, a marked increase in crimes of passion and motiveless murder was witnessed and, in Hampstead, Holborn and St Pancras, this proved no exception.

The first cases of death in Hampstead and St Pancras, due directly to war operations, were those of civilians dug out of bomb rubble following enemy air raids throughout September 1940. Unfortunately, bombed houses later proved to be convenient locations for local malevolents who used the ruins to commit murder and to dispose of their victims. Such an occurrence came to light when, on 13 October

*The wartime murder of Mabel Church topped the headlines alongside other crime related articles in the* St Pancras Chronicle, *17 October 1941.*

URDER MYSTERY OF BOMBED HOUSE

GIRL FOUND STRANGLED

OLITION WORKERS DISCOVERY

en engaged in the clearance of a bombed house in Hamp- oad, near Mornington Crescent, N.W.1, received a shock ey started work on Monday morning by finding among the e body of a partially clad girl who had apparently been . The girl was later identified as Mabel Church (19), of Road, N.7. Her jaw was bruised and round the neck was undergarment, while near the body was a cap, such as a might wear. Before the body was taken to St. Pancras it was examined by Sir Bernard Spilsbury, Pathologist, accompanied by Detective Superintendent Yandall and Divi- spector Clare, of New Scotland Yard, under whose direc- ger-print experts were for some time busily engaged.

NIGHT ARRESTS IN PARKWAY

ROOFS SEARCHED BY THE POLICE

William Henry Ellis (30), builder, of Arlington-road, N.W.1, and William John Worley (20), bricklayer, of Cropley-street N.1, were committed for trial by the Marylebone magistrate on a charge of breaking into premises in Parkway Camden Town, and stealing two typewriters, clothing, etc., worth £27, belonging to Messrs. Sims and Sims.

Albert Patten, foreman to the prosecutors, said he returned at about midnight and found the front door partly open. The door was obstructed with two of the firm's typewriters placed behind it. He called a fire watcher and told him to watch while he telephoned the police.

J.S. Inspector Peck said that with other officers he searched the York and Albany public-house without finding anyone. Other officers arrived and the premises were surrounded. He and P.C. Scott then climbed on to a

Liking For Fur Coats

Woman Who Stole Two Sentenced

Found guilty of stealing a silver fox fur cape, worth £39 18s., at the Berkeley Furs, Ltd., Edgware-road, W.2, and of stealing a silver fox fur coatee worth £35 from the premises of Allenby Ltd., Oxford-street, W.1, Catherine Baker (23), married, of Haverstock-street, City-road, who last week gave her maiden name Maloney and her mother's address at Carburton-street, W.1, was sentenced by Mr. L. R. Dunne at Marylebone Police Court to three months' imprisonment.

Queenie Winifred Heap, assistant to Messrs. Allenby, said accused came into the showroom and asked to see a silver fox bolero in the window. The accused found it was too small and witness went to get others. They did not suit accused, and she left, saying

FOUND GASSED AT OLD HOME

SUICIDE AFTER ROAD ACCIDENT

Involved in a motor-cycle accident on Sunday, October 5, Joseph Frederick Morris (54), a tailor's clerk, of Kemprow, Aldenham, Herts, was on Friday found gassed at a house in Cliff-road N.W.1, which he had occupied until it was blasted by enemy action.

At the inquest in St. Pancras on Tuesday Mr. Gordon Joseph Morris, of Harrow, said until the accident his father had always been a cheerful man and not easily upset. On October 5 his father was driving a motor-cycle combination with a passenger in the side-car and one on the pillion seat. While taking a left-hand bend the machine overturned owing to the pillion passenger leaning the wrong way. Both passengers were taken to hospital but his father, although badly shaken, escaped with a bruised elbow and refused medical aid.

On the following Wednesday witness was told his father was ill and refused

Notes Snatching Charge

"I Was Desperate" Says Accused

Bernard Cresswell Freeman (25), a clerk, no fixed home, was charged on remand before Mr. L. R. Dunne at Marylebone Police Court with stealing £29 in notes from the National Provincial Bank, Edgware-road, W.2, the money of the Aerated Bread Co. He pleaded guilty and was sent for trial at the Central Criminal Court.

Accused was arrested in a taxicab after, it was alleged, he had entered the bank, asked for a prospectus of National War Bonds, and snatched the notes.

Florence Kingham, manageress of the A.B.C., Edgware-road, said she had passed £35 in notes and silver over the counter at the bank when accused snatched the notes from over

DIFFICULTIES OF TRADERS

SUMMONSES DISMISSED BY MAGISTRATE

A plea of guilty was tendered on behalf of the London Co-operative Society at Clerkenwell on Tuesday to a summons for exposing for sale at Kentish Town-road, N.W.5, a clod of beef at 1s. 2d. per lb., the maximum price being ...

Mr. Hugh Jones, for the defence, said a ticket had been moved by mistake from another tray of meat.

The summons was dismissed under the Probation Act on payment of three guineas costs.

W. Bridger, trading as W. Bridger and Sons, of Seaton-place, N.W.1, pleaded guilty to exposing for sale imported best neck of lamb chops at 1s. 4d. per lb., the maximum price being 1s.

Defendant said his staff was depleted through war conditions, and at the time the employee who usually priced the meat was on holiday. A mistake was made by a man less familiar with

# Regent's Park Tragedy

---

## Verdict Of Murder Recorded

---

At the adjourned inquest at St. Pancras Coroner's Court on Thursday last week on Mrs. Edith Eleanor Humphries (50), a civilian cook in the A.F.S., of Gloucester-crescent, Regent's Park, N.W.1, who was found injured in bed on October 17 and died later at the National Temperance Hospital, a verdict of "Murder by some person or persons unknown was returned.

Mrs. Humphries was the widow of a cab proprietor.

Miss Jill Steele, who had lived above Mrs. Humphries, said that on October 17 she could not find her key and went downstairs to Mrs. Humphries to borrow hers. The door was open, and as she could get no reply she went into the room and flashed a torch on her face. She saw some blood. She had not found her key since.

Detective Inspector McDougall said there was no sign of forcible entry into Mrs. Humphries' apartment. There was a good amount of property, including a gold watch, in the place.

Sir Bernard Spilsbury said there had been attempted strangulation. Death was due to hemorrhage caused by a stab wound which penetrated the brain. It could have been caused by a knife with a sharp point and edge and a thick back.

1941, demolition workers entering a bombed house at 225 Hampstead Road, St Pancras, discovered the almost naked body of Mabel Church, a nineteen-year-old clerk from Tufnell Park. The post-mortem revealed that she had been strangled with her own cami-knickers. Contrary to the happy go lucky, 'girl next door' image she portrayed at work, her colleagues were shocked to find that Mabel enjoyed alcohol and frequently met servicemen for amorous liaisons. Earlier in the evening she had said goodnight to a girlfriend, Vera Whymark, at Charing Cross Station. Instead of returning home, Mabel met an unknown third party little knowing that only one hour later she would be dead. Between 9.45 pm and 10.00 pm, people living near the bombed house witnessed loud screams and even a soldier passing on a bus heard a shriek that to him was both very loud and unpleasant. Despite taking over two hundred witness statements, including a number of inconclusive leads involving errant servicemen, as well as an elaborate but bogus

*'A tragedy' is how the* St Pancras Chronicle *of 19 December 1941 described the motiveless and brutal murder of widow Edith Humphries. Her killer was never apprehended.*

confession by an army deserter in Stoke-on-Trent, the police could take the case no further. Mabel's murderer had simply vanished into the London blackout.

The Scotland Yard detectives who had been working day and night in an attempt to solve the murder of Mabel Church were to get little respite when, only a few days later, another foul deed was committed in St Pancras. This time they were called to investigate the death of Edith Eleanor Humphreys, a forty-eight-year-old widow and book-keeper for the auxiliary fire service, who resided at 1 Gloucester Crescent, Regent's Park. At 6.45 am on 17 October, Jill Steele, a fellow tenant, was drawn to Mrs Humphreys' two-roomed flat by the barking of the latter's pet terrier. Once inside, Miss Steele found the widow unconscious and badly beaten but miraculously still alive. Sadly, Mrs Humphreys was to die later in hospital from her injuries. She had not been robbed or sexually assaulted but had been attacked with excessive violence. Not only had the perpetrator attempted to strangle her but he had also broken her jaw in several places before finally stabbing her in the head with a sharp pointed object. A possible lead emerged following a search of the Gloucester Crescent flat. Detectives unearthed two letters penned by a fireman's wife; the first accused Mrs Humphreys of 'carrying on' with her husband but the second retracted the accusation. Upon interviewing the correspondent, police found the incident to be a misunderstanding and dropped it from their enquiries. This seemingly motiveless attack baffled the authorities and, as with the Church case, the absence of clues dictated that the investigation could not be taken any further.

Not all cases during the war years involved the murder of local women by anonymous killers. In April 1943, news headlines heralded a story of alleged fratricide. This case featured two brothers, Joseph and Israel Benjamin, one of whom fell from a moving train as it left Kentish Town West Station. On 25 April, forty-four-year-old Joseph, a fruiterer from Harrow, was travelling home with his older brother Israel in an empty carriage of a Broad Street to Wembley Train. The train was approximately five hundred yards from the station when Israel fell from the compartment to the tracks below. The communication cord was pulled and, when the train came to a halt, the guard attended to the badly injured man. Israel told the railway official that his brother had pushed him out of the train following a quarrel about the contents of their father's will. He exclaimed, 'he tried to rob me, my brother. He pushed me out. He tried to murder me … He is my brother.' Joseph, now at his brother's side, told the guard, 'I was asleep in the opposite corner. I did not know anything until I heard a bang, and then I pulled

# FATAL FALL FROM TRAIN

## BROTHER ON MURDER CHARGE

Joseph Benjamin (44), fruiterer, of Watford-road, Harrow, was at Clerkenwell Police Court on Monday remanded until May 10 charged with the murder of his brother Israel, who was said to have fallen from an electric train on Sunday.

Israel Benjamin, who was 45 and lived at Empire-road, Perivale, Middlesex, was, it is alleged, seen to fall from a Broad-street-Richmond train near Kentish Town (L.M.S.) Station.

Div. Det. Inspr. A. Slyfield said he saw Joseph Benjamin at Kentish Town police station and said to him: "I am going to charge you with the murder of your brother Israel Benjamin. You understand?"

Benjamin replied: "I understand."

When he was charged Benjamin said: "I am not guilty."

Inspector Slyfield asked for a remand.

Mr. Emanuel, for Benjamin, applied for bail and said: "He has given some explanation already of what has happened. I have not 'the slightest doubt when the proper time comes what the result will be."

The magistrate (Mr. Frank Powell): "Have you any special grounds for asking for bail?"

Mr. Emanuel: "I have no special grounds, but I am prepared to find very substantial sureties."

Mr. Powell said he was not prepared to grant bail.

Benjamin, who is tall and well built, was given a seat during the hearing, which lasted only a few minutes.

### Inquest Opened

Mr. W. Bentley Purchase, the St. Pancras Coroner, on Tuesday opened and adjourned until July 9 an inquest on Israel Benjamin, whose body was found on the L.M.S. Railway line near Kentish Town (West) Station on Sunday morning.

Evidence of identity was given by Jack Benjamin, a brother, of Methuen Park, Muswell Hill.

Dr. David Somerset Short, house surgeon at Hampstead General Hospital, said when brought there at 11.30 a.m. the man was dead.

Sir Bernard Spilsbury, who made the post-mortem examination, said the body was that of a stoutly-built and generally speaking healthy man. There was a lacerated wound 2¾ in. long on the top of the head, the left arm was fractured and abrasions and bruises were distributed about the left hip, both thighs and the right hand. Internally there was a depressed fracture of the skull beneath the wound on the top of the head, but the brain was not injured. All the ribs on the left side were fractured, as were the first nine on the right. There were also crushing of the spinal cord and a fractured pelvis. The cause of death was hemorrhage due to multiple injuries.

Answering the Coroner, Sir Bernard said there was no reason, as the brain was not injured, why the man should not have been mentally alert and capable until loss of blood caused unconsciousness.

Detective Inspector Daykin, of N Division, said Joseph Benjamin, a brother of the dead man, had been charged at Clerkenwell Police Court in connection with the death and stood remanded in custody.

At this stage the Coroner said that assuming the matter went to the Central Criminal Court, he would adjourn his inquiry in case he had to go on with it, until July 9.

The police desire to get into touch with a man who alighted from a L.M.S. Broad-street to Richmond electric train when it arrived at Kentish Town (West) Station at 10.15 a.m. on Sunday. It is believed that this man was in the same compartment in which the dead man and his brother travelled.

*Joseph Benjamin was later acquitted of the murder of his brother, Israel, who fell to his death from a moving train in Kentish Town. Article taken from the* St Pancras Chronicle, *April 30 1943.*

the emergency cord.' Police Inspector Willmott quickly arrived at the scene and questioned Israel further. The injured party explained how the recent will favoured Joseph above himself and their other brothers, 'we quarrelled over it in the train.' Israel said that his brother declared, 'You won't get nothing. You have got to work [but in reply] I said I want my half share. He called me no good. He got me by the neck and pushed me out.' An ambulance came to take Israel to hospital but he died a little later from multiple injuries. Given Israel Benjamin's dying statement, the police had no choice but to charge Joseph with his brother's murder. Upon his arrest, the fruiterer accused his diseased brother of being 'the biggest liar out!' Joseph Benjamin and his defence were able to reveal the truth at his two-day trial that began on 25 May at the Old Bailey. The court heard the background to the brothers' relationship. Joseph was hard working and conscientious whereas Israel was excitable and neurotic. Relations between the two took a turn for the worse following the reading of their late father's will. Israel believed that Joseph had been left a greater share, and in the presence of their solicitor announced, 'I have nothing to live for ... I will do myself in.' Another brother, Jack, told of Israel's difficult nature and that, in actuality, it was Joseph who came to his rescue when Israel was ejected from his father's house. The family doctor also testified that the deceased suffered from delusions. It could be inferred therefore, though not proved, that Israel flung himself from the train whilst in an agitated state. Not surprisingly, the jury took just two minutes to find Joseph not guilty. After the verdict was read, Joseph left the court to say a prayer over his brother's grave.

Women victims were regrettably not out of the headlines for long but it appeared that little sympathy was afforded those females who came to a bad end whilst undertaking their 'national service' as prostitutes. With demand high, especially in the capital, many were practising the age-old trade for the first time: the number of women working the streets is said to have doubled during the war years. A night's work could be financially rewarding but the risks were equally high. Yorkshire-born Jean Stafford was in her early thirties when she decided to supplement her income from pub work with money earned from prostitution. With her good looks and friendly way with customers (pub and otherwise), Jean was more than able to look after her own needs. That was until her untimely death possibly at the hands of a client on 19 May 1942. By this time, she had given up her day job to concentrate entirely on the 'nightshift'. She used a flat rented for her by a book-maker known as 'Johnnie' in Bedford Place, Holborn. On the morning of 19 May, landlady Edith O'Connor had found Jean dead on her bed, wearing only a brassiere. Apart from her face appearing slightly flushed, there was no immediate indication that a violent struggle had taken place. Her flat was neat and tidy and there were no signs of a second person having been present. The post-mortem proved otherwise. It revealed that Jean had been strangled by a ligature pulled tightly around her neck; the ligature had been improvised from the discarded dress she had been wearing. It was established that her death had occurred between 8.00 pm and 9.00 pm on the night before her body was discovered. Fellow residents reported hearing Jean converse with a man in the Bedford Place dwelling earlier that evening. Furthermore, doors were heard slamming in the early hours of the next morning. Evidently, the killer had waited a few hours before making an unseen exit. Suspects included the mysterious 'Johnnie', who couldn't be traced after her death, as well as a man who Jean had arranged to meet in a pub earlier that evening. At the inquest into her death, a verdict of murder by some person or persons unknown was justifiably recorded and, despite interviewing up to one hundred people in connection with the case, the police never caught her killer. But, not all murders of known prostitutes went unsolved or involved 'shadowy' suspects.

A bombed house in Kilburn Priory, Hampstead, provided the scene for the murder of Mrs Sarah Gwendoline Parry, a forty-year-old local waitress and part-time prostitute. On this occasion, in late September 1944, the authorities spent little time investigating her death. Shortly after her body was discovered, the killer surrendered himself to the police, accompanied by his mother! Confessing all was Irish electrician Louis Walsh, three years the junior of his victim. Mrs Parry had casually met Walsh one evening in the *Priory Tavern*, a hostelry located at the Kilburn end of Belsize Road. After a number of drinks, presumably during which a fee was negotiated, Mrs Parry led her client to a bombed house for sex. On arrival, and with the aid of torches, the two settled on an old leather couch and, at this point, Mrs Parry asked to see the 'colour' of Walsh's money before proceeding.[29] According to Walsh,

*She said she wanted the money first and began to scream. I clapped my hand over her mouth when she wouldn't stop and then with my right fist struck her a number of heavy blows about the face and head … I might have had the torch in my hand when I was striking her, but I don't remember.*

After the attack the Irishman staggered off and headed for a café in Swiss Cottage called the *Hole in the Wall*. His face and shirt were

# MURDER VERDICT RETURNED

---

## POLICE SEEK A MAN NAMED "JOHNNIE"

At the resumed inquest at St. Pancras Coroner's Court on Friday on Mrs. Agnes (or Jean) Stafford (33), wife of an A.R.P. warden in Leeds, who was found strangled at her flat in Bedford-place, W.C.1, on May 19, the jury returned a verdict of "Murder by some person or persons unknown."

Mrs. Edith O'Connor, a housekeeper, said on several occasions she had admitted a man called "Johnnie" to the house to see Mrs. Stafford, but he was the only man she had ever let in. "Johnnie" had neither called nor telephoned since the woman's death.

Joseph Lamb, the occupier of a flat in the same house, said he had dinner with a man called "Alec" in Mrs. Stafford's room a few weeks before her death, but had not seen him since.

Sir Bernard Spilsbury said that Mrs. Stafford's death was due to asphyxia caused through strangulation by a ligature which had been tied tightly round her neck. Her jaw had been broken, and there was severe bruising all over her body, probably resulting from a struggle. There were also signs that her neck had been grasped by a hand which may have rendered her unconscious while the ligature, of some soft material, like a dress, was tightened.

Detective Inspector Rudkin said in the course of inquiries statements had been taken by the police from over 100 people.

In connection with the death the police have issued a description of a man known as "Johnnie" whom they want to interview. He is of the "dapper" type, 30 to 40 years of age, 5ft. 4in. in height, thin build, thin-faced, with a long nose and fair complexion. Anyone who recognizes the description and can assist the police to trace "Johnnie" is asked to get in touch with Supt. Rees or Div. Det. Inspr. Rudkin at Bow-street Police Station.

bloodied but he let staff believe that he had been involved in a pub fight. Later, and feeling remorseful, he confessed all to his landlady. He told her that he couldn't remember if he had hit Sarah or not, as he was too mad and too drunk, but he was adamant that she was still breathing when he left her. Mrs Parry's battered body was found the next morning and that evening an account of her death was reported in the press. Walsh realised that the body discovered was that of the woman with whom he had been with the previous evening. Experiencing further guilt, he attended confession at the Roman Catholic Church of the Sacred Heart in Quex Road before again confessing his sins to the police. Louis Walsh was sentenced to twenty-one months' imprisonment for manslaughter; a verdict and sentence that clearly placed little value on his victim's life.

The trials and tribulations of war also led to several cases of suicide and, in one case in St Pancras, a suicide pact that ended in tragedy. Margaret Sarah Hayward was a married mother of two living in Windsor House, a large block of flats located in Cumberland Market near Regent's Park. Whilst her able seaman husband was away serving his country, the lonely housewife took a younger lover named Herbert Robert John Macavoy. As a plumber who was declared unfit for national service, the twenty-two-year-old conveniently

*Despite publicity generated by this article in the* Holborn Guardian *of 26 June 1942, 'Johnnie' was never found and Jean Stafford's murder went unsolved.*

lived in the same block as Mrs Hayward. After a while, their affair blossomed and Hayward decided to tell her husband upon his return that she wanted to leave him for Macavoy. Meanwhile, for the sake of the children, the liaison was to remain a secret. The plumber became tired with the underhand nature of their association and suggested to his lover that they should end it. He did not mean for them to part company but instead for them to take their relationship several levels higher by committing double suicide. The besotted Mrs Hayward agreed wholeheartedly to this and declared, 'on no account must you leave me behind.' The following night Macavoy again discussed the proposition with her and still she was in no doubt. At his dictation Mrs Hayward wrote a suicide note on his behalf to show her commitment and, in return, he added a postscript also promising to see it though: 'My own darling Madge, pray God I have courage to do my share.'

The couple had initially decided on the evening of 14 March 1944 on which to perform the deed but the night-time arrival of the Luftwaffe caused its postponement. Incendiary bombs destroyed the top two floors of

# Man Accused of Murder in Kilburn

## "I Have Come to Give Myself Up."

*Louis Christopher Walsh, aged 37, electrician, of Fordwych Road, West Hampstead, was charged at the Marylebone Police Court on Monday, before Mr. Ronald Powell, with the murder of Sarah Gwendoline Parry, at a bomb-damaged house in Kilburn Priory.*

Div. Det. Inspector John Smale said at 9.40 a.m. on September 23, he saw the accused at West Hampstead Police Station and told him he understood he wished to tell him something about a woman who was found dead at Kilburn Priory on Thursday last. Accused said "Yes, sir. I didn't know she was dead until last night. I have seen a priest this morning, and now I have come to give myself up. I must tell you all about it."

### "I LOST MY HEAD."

"I asked 'What do you want to tell me?'" said the inspector. "He said he met a woman in the Priory Tavern a week previously. He had never seen her before. She took him to a bombed house near the tavern."

Walsh's alleged statement to the detective continued: "She asked for £1, and when I told her I hadn't as much as £1, she bit me and began to scream. I tried to stop her by holding her mouth, but she would not stop and I got frightened and hit her. Then I lost my head and hit her a lot and when she was unconscious I ran out of the house. I have been watching the papers ever since in case she complained to the police."

Witness, said he told the accused he would be detained for further inquiries. At 2.30 p.m. the same day he saw him again and cautioned him, and said "I am now ready to listen to anything you wish to tell me." The accused said "I must tell you everything to get it off my mind or I will go mad. I didn't mean to hurt her, only to stop her screaming."

### SIGNED STATEMENT.

Inspector Smale said the accused made a statement under caution which was written down and signed. He didn't proposed to put it in at this stage.

At 6.35 p.m., he continued, the accused was charged with the murder of Sarah Gwendoline Parry, and he said "What can I say? I want to say this much: this woman has died as a result of my actions, but I had no intention of killing her."

In reply to the magistrate the accused said he had nothing to say at this stage.

The accused was remanded for 14 days at the request of the inspector on the ground that there were a number of inquiries yet to be made and for the papers to be placed before the Director of Public Prosecutions.

The magistrate certified for a counsel and solicitor to defend the accused.

### Dead Several Days—Doctor's Evidence at Inquest

At the inquest at St. Pancras on Monday, Mrs. Parry's age was given as 40.

Her husband, Mr. Garfield Parry, of Penfold Street, N.W.8, said his wife lived at Springfield Lane, Kilburn. He last saw her two months ago.

Dr. Stephen J. Knight, police divisional surgeon, Willesden Lane, said he was called to a house in Kilburn Priory on September 21 and saw the body of a woman who appeared to have been dead several days. Her face, which was covered with blood, appeared to have been battered. There were bloodstains on her clothing, arms and legs, while her lips were bruised and lacerated.

Sir Bernard Spilsbury, pathologist who made the post mortem examination, said death was caused by shock due to multiple head injuries. He agreed with Dr. Knight that the woman had been dead some little time, although it was difficult to fix the exact period. As the place where the body was found was cold and dark, he added, it might have been there a few days.

The inquest was adjourned until November 20th.

*The killer, Louis Walsh, first confessed his guilt in church and then confessed all to the local police. Article taken from the* Kilburn Times, *29 September 1944.*

*Windsor House, Cumberland Market, c.1953. This Crown Estate block was once home to Margaret Hayward, 'the woman who agreed to be murdered'.*

Windsor House but rather than take advantage of the flames, to assist their own fateful end, Mrs Hayward and Macavoy bade each other goodnight. He returned to his parent's flat further along the balcony and she spent the remainder of the evening with her cousin, Lily Stewart, in Gower Street. The following day Mrs Hayward arranged to evacuate her son to relatives in Swansea, after which she returned to her flat in Cumberland Market. No raid occurred that night so the two were able to spend the time together until the next morning, now 16 March. Macavoy was, however, still very much intent on carrying out the suicide pact. In fact, after waking, he chose that same morning to raise the subject again with Margaret. He casually inquired if she still wanted to go ahead with what she had agreed to do a few nights earlier, to which she simply replied, 'Yes.' Then after a while, according to Macavoy, 'I took her by the throat with my hands and choked her. She made no sound and did not struggle.' She had clearly gone through with her side of the arrangement and now, as they'd agreed, it was

Macavoy's turn to join her in the hereafter. He had no clear idea of how or when he would perform his share but, for the time being, he acted as if nothing at all had happened. After tidying up, he left a message to Lily Stewart attached to the front door of Mrs Hayward's flat; rather inappropriately it was written on the back of an old 'In Memoriam' card. He instructed her not to go into her cousin's bedroom and further requested her to burn his letters to Madge and not to make it hard on Vic (Mrs Hayward's husband). He then left and reported to his employer, Mr Pike. Under the burden of guilt, Macavoy confessed to Mr Pike, 'I have just strangled Mrs Hayward', after which he broke down and wept. As Mr Pike phoned the police, Macavoy pushed past his employer and dashed from the premises. He ran to a nearby tube station, where he thought of throwing himself under a train but, instead, he travelled to Camden Town. Macavoy then took a taxi to Belsize Park where he changed cabs and headed back to Windsor House. En route he requested that the cabbie to stop at a public house so that he could partake of some 'dutch courage'. Upon arrival at Windsor House, Macavoy was met by Mr Pike and Detective Inspector Clare to whom he quietly surrendered, declaring, 'It's all right I know what you want me for. My God! My poor Marjorie.' Escorting him to nearby Albany Street Police Station, DI Clare heard another admission of guilt from his prisoner, 'She is dead. I did it with my own hands. What a mess I am in.' The post-mortem concurred with Macavoy's confession to find that the cause of death was indeed manual strangulation. The jury at Macavoy's trial returned a verdict of murder against the feckless plumber. He was sentenced to death on 28 April 1944 but a month later the Home Secretary recommended a reprieve. As well as being yet another example of senseless murder in a time when, for some, normality and morality were suspended, this case will also be remembered for Herbert Macavoy, the killer of 'the woman who agreed to be murdered'.

# CHAPTER 19

# Weapons of Choice
## 1949–50

*… it would not be the last time that a sword was used to kill in the area.*

In the years following the Second World War, residents of Hampstead, Holborn and St Pancras began to rebuild their lives and homes again. Yet, this post-war rebuilding did little to convince some elements in society that crime did not pay and was not welcome. Between 1948 and 1950, eighty-nine murders were committed within the London Metropolitan area alone.[30] Seemingly the horrors experienced between 1939 and 1945 had little effect on those still intent on committing this foulest of deeds.

Early August 1949 witnessed two such deeds. Perhaps the most abhorrent of all crime is the murder of a child. Even today, murder against children is relatively rare and even rarer when the perpetrator is a woman but that summer a story emerged that was to sicken the country. On 12 August, just thirty hours after three-year-old Marian

# GIRL FOUND BATTERED TO DEATH

## Woman Charged With Murder

### Man's Skeleton Discovered In Search For Child

AFTER COMBING THE DISTRICT FOR THIRTY HOURS, POLICE FOUND THREE-YEAR-OLD MARIAN MARGARET WARD BATTERED TO DEATH IN A BOMBED HOUSE AT THE CORNER OF AVENUE ROAD AND St. JOHN'S WOOD PARK, N.W.8, ON SATURDAY NIGHT, ABOUT A QUARTER OF A MILE FROM HER HOME IN ELSWORTHY ROAD, N.W.3.

AT ALBANY STREET POLICE STATION, N.W.1, ON MONDAY NIGHT, Mrs. NORA PATRICIA TIERNEY (29), OF ELSWORTHY ROAD, WAS CHARGED WITH THE MURDER OF THE CHILD. SHE WAS BROUGHT BEFORE THE MARYLEBONE MAGISTRATE ON TUESDAY AND REMANDED IN CUSTODY.

DURING THEIR SEARCH FOR MARIAN, SCOTLAND YARD DETECTIVES FOUND THE SKELETON OF A MAN, FULLY DRESSED, UNDER THE BASEMENT STAIRS OF A BOMBED HOUSE IN ADELAIDE ROAD, N.W.3.

*The tragic and senseless murder of three-year-old Marian Ward, as reported in the* Holborn Guardian, *19 August 1949.*

Ward disappeared, her little battered body was found in the ruins of Langham Court, Avenue Road, Hampstead. The bomb-damaged residence was situated only four hundred yards from Marian's home in Elsworthy Road. She had been the victim of a brutal assault; the murder weapon of choice was a hammer, later found hidden in a heap of soil and stones just inside Primrose Hill at its Elsworthy Road entrance. Officially, little Marian's death was from 'shock and haemorrhage due to injuries to the brain from a fractured skull.' During the search for the child, the police also found the remains of a fully dressed man in the same house in which they were to find Marian. The male body had been dead up to six months. Meanwhile, it was not long until a suspect was charged with Marian's murder. This was twenty-nine-year-old, Irish-born Nora Patricia Tierney, who was next-door neighbour to the Ward family. At her two-day trial commencing on 17 October 1949, Tierney pleaded her innocence and blamed her long-suffering husband James for the deed. There was no evidence to suggest that he had any involvement in the murder, whereas forensics showed that the accused had been in recent, close contact with Marian. Mr Tierney also gave evidence against his wife by testifying that during the night, after the murder occurred, he was awakened by his wife who confessed to him that she had hit Marian on the head with a hammer. He also confirmed that the murder weapon was theirs and was usually kept in their kitchen. Not surprisingly, Nora Tierney was found guilty of the crime and sentenced to death. Her appeal also failed. The Lord Chief Justice intimated that if she had initially pleaded insanity then this would have been taken into consideration. He went on to comment, 'it might be said that anybody committing the murder must have been insane, because a more motiveless murder could not be imagined.' For this 'insane' murder, Nora Tierney was to be executed on 30 November 1949, leaving behind her own six-year-old daughter. In a final twist, the prison doctors concluded that she was indeed suffering from abnormality of mind and, instead of hanging, she was committed to Broadmoor Hospital for the criminally insane.

A few days after poor Marian Ward was murdered in Hampstead, reports of a murder in Holborn were filtering through. This time a thirty-six-year-old secretarial agent, Dorothy Wallis, was found stabbed to death in her third floor back office. But unlike Marian's killer, the murderer of Miss Wallis was never caught. Described as tall, reserved and very pleasant, the victim ran the Adelphi Secretarial Agency at 157 High Holborn. This was located near to Holborn Town Hall, opposite the opening to Smart's Buildings. Just after 9 am on Tuesday, 16 August, her body was found by Shelia Bennett, an employee who had been with the agency for just one day! Miss Wallis was covered in blood and lying on her back just behind the door. Shocked at the sight, Miss Bennett ran screaming from the office looking for assistance; she initially thought that her employer had suffered a lung haemorrhage. There were no signs of robbery but the office furniture was in disarray and the telephone handset was hanging on its flex. Clearly a violent struggle had taken place. It appeared that Dorothy had been stabbed twice in the left side of her chest, with the wounds penetrating her heart. She had also been stabbed four times in the back and there was a five-inch gash on her arm. The police theorised that she knew her killer and that his hands could have been badly cut in the attack.

*Miss Dorothy Wallis. Despite an extensive investigation, her killer was never brought to justice.*

Leading the investigation was Chief Superintendent Harold Hawkyard. He and his team searched the building for over seven hours but failed to find a murder weapon. The post-mortem revealed that death was caused by stab wounds with a sharp pointed knife and the time of death was given to be between 6 pm and 7 pm the previous evening. The police attempted to piece together the last hour or so of Dorothy Wallis's life leading up to her murder. At about 5.50 pm, Miss Wallis had bid goodnight to one of her prospective temps, Joyce Jones; strangely, the young secretary had a premonition that something was going to happen and reported this to her mother when she arrived home. Fifteen or so minutes later, Iris Wilkins, another temp, had rang the office looking to speak to Dorothy only to be taken by surprise when the telephone was answered by a man. In an educated but brusque voice, the man explained that Miss Wallis had left for the evening and suggested that she ring earlier next time. A little while later, neighbour Rose Crowley said that just

*154-159 High Holborn prior to demolition in 1957. The street entrance to Dorothy Wallis's office was the fourth door from the right of the picture (beneath the double drainpipe). The entrance to Dunn's Passage can be seen to the extreme right.*

before 7.00 pm she heard a woman scream, 'Don't murder me.' A further clue emerged when witnesses came forward to tell of a man seen running along nearby Dunn's Passage at about 6.15 pm. His description was that of a swarthy looking, sturdily built man of Italian appearance aged between twenty-five and thirty years. He stood about 5′ 5″ tall with long dark hair brushed back and sideburns. Unfortunately, despite this detailed account, Chief Superintendent Hawkyard never managed to locate the anonymous sprinter. Another

# Student Found Stabbed

## Butler On Murder Charge

Yesterday, at Clerkenwell, Socrates Petrides (32), a wine butler, of Gray's Inn-road, W.C.1, was charged with the murder on or about Wednesday, at that address, of Fred Hardisty.

The police had found Hardisty, a 20-year-old student, of Devonshire-road, Blackpool, stabbed to death early on Wednesday.

Det.-Inspector Cecil Hodgins told the court that at 6 p.m. on August 9 he saw Petrides at Gray's Inn-road police station and said to him:—

"In the early hours of this morning I saw the dead body of Fred Hardisty at your address at 57, Gray's Inn-road. As a result of inquiries I have since made I am going to charge you with murdering him."

Petrides replied: "Yes, sir, I understand. I have told you all about it. I cannot say more."

Petrides was a Cypriot, said the officer, but he understood English.

Asked by the magistrate (Mr. Frank Powell) if he had any questions to ask the officer, Petrides replied: "No, sir."

He was remanded in custody until next Friday, and granted a legal aid certificate.

*A fatal mis-understanding in which the butler actually did it! Article taken from the* Holborn Guardian, *11 August 1950.*

person the police were eager to trace was a Polish man who had come to the agency earlier in the day 'desperately' looking for work. Could he have returned at the end of the working day and argued with Dorothy Wallis, which led to her murder?

During the course of the investigation it appeared that Miss Wallis took a deep interest in men and was a frequent visitor to the Overseas Club. She also kept secret diaries in shorthand but these were so cryptic

*57 Gray's Inn Road, Holborn, in 2004.*

that the police could make little use of them. Over six hundred statements were taken during the enquiry but all counted for nothing as no arrest was ever made. Apart from the identity of the killer, one further crucial element evaded police detection, as is so often in cases of this nature, and that was motive. Exactly why was she murdered? Had she simply met an overseas gentleman for pleasure that turned nasty? Or, did the disagreement with the unemployed Pole ultimately lead to her demise? And who was the 'educated' gentleman who answered her telephone? Was his the voice of the killer? Just what drove someone to kill Miss Wallis will, alas, remain unanswered but the mystery surrounding the absent murder weapon may have been solved some eight years later. A sword found during demolition of 157 High Holborn and adjacent buildings in 1957 would have been more than capable of causing the secretarial agent's injuries. The doubled edged weapon measured about four feet in length and was discovered behind boxes of rubbish in a room just three or four doors away from the scene of the murder. Whether it was the instrument that brought about the death of Dorothy Wallis was never confirmed but, if it were the weapon of choice, it would not be the last time that a sword was used to kill in the area.

A sword also proved to be the weapon of choice in an incident occurring in Holborn just twelve months later. In August 1950, thirty-two-year old Cypriot wine waiter, Socrates Petrides, was charged with the murder of student Fred Hardisty. Petrides had become friendly with the twenty-year-old Hardisty in one of Soho's homosexual cafes, the latter apparently not realising the nature of the establishment. On 9 August, having missed his train home to Blackpool, Hardisty was offered shelter for the night by Petrides in his small top floor flat at 57 Gray's Inn Road. The young student clearly misunderstood his host's intentions and, when Petrides made sexual advances, a fight between the two ensued. In the struggle, the waiter grabbed an ornamental samurai sword to fend off the furious Hardisty but instead ended up killing him. Petrides was charged with murder but, at his trial, he was found guilty only of manslaughter. The Cypriot's conviction was one of many that heralded the arrival of foul deeds for the new decade. This proved to be a violent period that witnessed a number of infamous, local cases, including the high profile conviction and execution of Ruth Ellis, the last woman in England to be hanged.

# CHAPTER 20

# The Last Women to be Hanged in Britain
## 1954–55

*To them (her sympathisers), she was a woman driven over the edge.*

Following her short trial in October 1954, the populace agreed that Styllou Pantopiou Christofi was truly 'the mother-in-law from hell'. The fifty-three-year old Cypriot National was convicted and sentenced to death for the murder of her thirty-six-year-old daughter-in-law, Hella Dorothea Christofis, earlier the same year. During the legal proceedings, it emerged that Styllou Christofi was a possessive, domineering and insanely jealous woman who, embittered by the hardships in her own life, saw to it that no one else should enjoy a happiness that she herself was denied.

Born in an arid Cypriot village, Styllou's early life had been difficult. Her husband was one of the poorest men in the village and what little money they earned came from a tiny olive grove. Their life became even more desperate when Styllou stood trial for the murder of her own mother-in-law in 1925. Witnesses testified that she forced a flaming torch down her mother-in-law's throat causing her death. Astonishingly, Styllou was acquitted of the charge and walked free from court. Her only son, Stavros, also added to her misery by leaving home to work as a waiter in Nicosia. By 1941, Stavros Christofi had saved enough money to book passage on a boat bound for England. He quickly settled down and later obtained a job as a wine waiter at the prestigious *Café de Paris* in London's West End. The hard working Cypriot married flaxen-haired Hella, a German fashion model, who later bore him three healthy children. The family home was located on the fringes of Hampstead Heath at 11 South Hill Park. Unfortunately, their prosperous and tranquil existence was soon to be shattered by the arrival of Hella's mother-in-law, the 'demonic' Styllou.

The young couple understood that adapting to life in a major world city from a rural Mediterranean environment would be difficult for any rational person let alone for someone with Styllou's temperament and resentment. Stavros and his wife tried every which way they could to integrate Styllou into both their family and into an English way of life but, from the outset, she took an instant dislike to her new lifestyle and, especially, to her daughter-in-law. Styllou constantly criticized Hella's parenting skills and regularly flew into tantrums when denied her own way. In desperation, Hella issued an ultimatum to her husband. She was to take her children to Germany on holiday, insisting that he send Styllou back to Cyprus before her return. Unbeknown to Stavros, his mother came up with her own radical solution. She would simply eradicate Hella, using the same vehemence used to eliminate her own mother-in-law some thirty years earlier. Little did Stavros know, therefore, of the horror that was to unfold following his departure for work on the evening of Thursday, 29 July 1954.

With the children safely in bed, Styllou began to execute a plan that she believed would guarantee her everlasting happiness with her son and grandchildren. Selecting the kitchen as the location in

*Mrs Styllou Christofi, the archetypal 'mother-in-law from hell' and the penultimate woman to be hanged in Britain. Portrait drawn by Rachel Dilworth from a contemporary photograph.*

which to perform the monstrous deed, Mrs Christofi first knocked her daughter-in-law unconscious with a crashing blow to the back of her head using a cast iron ash plate from the stove. Moving swiftly, she then wound a scarf around Hella's neck and twisted the ligature until there was no life left within. Lastly, and seemingly not simply content with murder by strangulation, Styllou created a homemade funeral pyre in the back yard of the house in a doomed attempt to obliterate all traces of her victim, as well as the crime. As the fire enveloped Hella's lifeless corpse, the flames caught the attention of next-door neighbour John Young. Believing the house to be ablaze, Mr Young peered into his neighbour's yard only to be stunned by the sight of what appeared to be a 'tailor's dummy' being burned; he later recounted that it never occurred to him that it was a human body. Then, upon seeing Hella's

*As this article from the* Hampstead and Highgate Express *(6 August 1954) demonstrates, the cold bloodied murder of Hella Christofis attracted great local interest.*

# Did not use petrol, says mother-in-law

Mrs. Styllou Christofi, 53, a Cypriot, of South Hill Park, Hampstead, made her second appearance at Hampstead on Wednesday charged with murdering her daughter-in-law, Mrs. Hella Christofis, who was found strangled and burnt on her kitchen doorstep in South Hill Park, Hampstead, last Thursday. She was remanded in custody until next Friday and granted legal aid.

mother-in-law emerge from the house to tend the fire, Mr Young accepted the somewhat surreal scene and returned inside. At around 1 am, in an obvious attempt to cover up what she had done, Mrs Christofi ran into the street and flagged down the car of a local restaurant manager, Mr Burstoff, on his way home with his wife. In broken English she pleaded for his help, 'Please come. Fire burning. Children sleeping.' Accompanying the panic stricken woman back to the scene of the fire, he too saw the charred remains of what appeared to be a mannequin. Although the fire was now extinguished, Mr Burstoff justifiably raised the alarm.

Accompanying the police were St Pancras Coroner William Bentley Purchase and forensic pathologist Dr Francis Camps. The investigating party briefly examined the charred body and, upon seeing the condition of the throat and the smashed skull, deduced that the death was suspicious and not as a result of fire; the ensuing post-mortem at St Pancras Mortuary confirmed their deductions. Meanwhile, detectives had already started questioning Styllou Christofi and it was not long before

Mr. H. J. Rustomji, a Cypriot barrister on holiday in this country, told the bench: "I appear for this poor, unfortunate illiterate woman who is a stranger in our midst."

Making an application for legal aid for her he said his instructions were that she was destitute and had no money at all.

### Charge translated

Mrs. Christofi, who wore a check coat over a grey dress, stood with her arms folded while the charge was translated into Greek for her by an interpreter.

Giivng evidence of arrest Detective Superintendent Leonard Crawford said he saw Mrs. Christofi at Hampstead police station on 29 July and told her she would be charged with the murder of her daughter-in-law.

When she was charged she said, "I did not make use of any petrol but some few days previously some petrol spilled on the floor. I did not pay any attention to it.

"I stepped on it and perhaps the smell was the result of the petrol. From this story I know nothing more."

## INQUEST WAS ADJOURNED

Formal evidence of identification was given at last Friday's opening of the inquest on Mrs. Christofis.

Dr. F. E. Camps, pathologist: I am in the process of conducting lengthy postmortem investigations which are not yet complete.

The coroner: I shall resume this inquest earlier if you wish but in the meantime I shall adjourn it until 24 August.

evidence against her was gathered, leading to her arrest for murder. The horrific details of her ill conceived and vindictive plot to rid herself of Hella were fully exposed at her trial, which began a little under three months later in October. In her defence, Styllou Christofi argued that on the fateful night she was awoken by the smell of smoke. She rushed into Hella's room only to find it empty. Then running downstairs she came across her daughter-in-law in the back yard engulfed in flames. Mrs Christofi told the court how she attempted to splash water over Hella to quench the fire but on finding this ineffective she ran into the street for help and found the Burstoffs. In some versions of her account, she also alleged that two men had committed the crime. As earlier described, the true story of events on 29 July ran somewhat differently to Mrs Christofi's bogus narrative. In identifying her as the murderer, the police offered evidence in the form of the bloodstained kitchen, paraffin soaked newspapers and rags, Hella's head injuries and ligature marks upon her neck, and, perhaps most incriminating of all, the discovery of her daughter-in-law's wedding ring wrapped and hidden behind a vase in her own bedroom.

It was an undemanding task for the jury to find Styllou Christofi guilty of this insane murder. Perhaps, if insanity was initially pleaded as reason for murder, then the obligatory death sentence would have been almost certainly avoided. The court, however, deemed Styllou bad but not mad. In fact, she herself feared being labelled insane and made this clear at her trial, 'I am a poor woman, of no education, but I am not [a] mad woman. Never. Never. Never!' Naturally, there was little public sympathy for the middle-aged Cypriot after sentence of death was passed. Even Stavros shunned his mother. He neither visited her in the condemned cell nor attempted to save her from the gallows. Nevertheless, as the day of execution in December drew near, a campaign to seek her reprieve gathered momentum. The last woman to be previously hanged for murder was Edith Thompson some thirty years earlier, so there appeared to be good cause for hope. The Home Secretary thought otherwise and refused to advise the Queen to exercise her royal prerogative of mercy. Following Styllou Christofi's execution by hangman Albert Pierrepoint on 15 December 1954 at Holloway Prison, there was much 'disquiet' amongst members in the House of Commons. A group of Labour MPs tabled a motion seeking an urgent review of the decision not to exercise clemency. They also called for re-evaluation of the law surrounding capital punishment. Yet, it was to take one more murder, again in South Hill Park, namely the shooting of David Blakely by Ruth Ellis in 1955, for these matters to be seriously considered by Parliament. Indeed, the controversy

# RACING CAR DRIVER SHOT IN THE BACK

## Model for trial on murder charge

BLOOD-STAINED CLOTHING, A .38 REVOLVER, TWO BULLETS AND SIX CART-RIDGE CASES WERE PRODUCED IN THE CROWDED COURTROOM AT HAMPSTEAD YESTERDAY WHEN SILVER-HAIRED MODEL MRS. RUTH ELLIS, 28, OF EGERTON GARDENS, KENSINGTON, WAS SENT FOR TRIAL TO THE OLD BAILEY ON A CHARGE OF MURDER.

She is alleged to have shot and killed racing motorist 25-year-old David Blakely outside the Magdala Tavern, South Hill Park, Hampstead, on Easter Sunday.

Sixteen witnesses gave evidence at the all-day hearing.

Still wearing the two-piece grey suit she wore at her two previous appearances, Mrs. Ellis sat calmly in the dock throughout the 6½ hours. She showed no emotion at all.

The alleged shooting was described by Mr. Bertram Clive Gunnell, motor salesman, of South Hill Park, who was with Blakely when he died.

He said he went with Blakely to the flat of a friend, Mr. Anthony Findlater, in Tanza Road, Hampstead, on Easter Sunday and after two hours they left to get some beer from the Magdala.

"We had a drink each and bought three more quarts. I left the public house ahead of Blakely. I went round the front of his car to get in the passenger door. Then I heard two bangs.

"I heard somebody run and shout, 'Clive.' I ran round the back. I saw David lying on the pavement and Mrs. Ellis firing a gun. She was pointing it at his back. He was lying on his stomach, curled up with his head on his right arm."

Mr. Gunnell said he had no idea how many shots she fired—it was more than one.

Mrs. Ellis, he alleged, then said, "Now go and call the police."

Cross-examined by Mr. Sebag

Shaw, defending, he said the first thing he heard was two bangs.

"They didn't sound to me like revolver shots but something deeper and more muffled. David was lying in the middle of the pavement and never moved after I first saw him. Mrs. Ellis was standing at David's feet between him and the public house. I saw her firing for a second or two. Then it was all over."

Mrs. Gladys Yule, or Parliament Hill, Hampstead, said she was walking down Parliament Hill with her husband towards the public house. She saw two young men coming out of the public house door with a woman in front of them.

### SAW A FLASH

"I saw a flash and heard a shot. Then I saw a young man trying to get into the car parked at the kerb. He didn't get in but ran round the car. The lady chased him. There was another shot. He staggered round the car and fell.

There were two more shots. He was flat out then."

Mrs. Yale said the shots were accompanied by flashes which came from the woman's hand.

"After the last flash I had a searing pain through my right hand," she said.

PC Alan Thompson said he was off duty in the saloon bar at the Magdala when he saw two men he now knew to be Gunnell and Blakely come in. He noticed a fair-haired woman wearing spectacles looking through the window.

"About five minutes later I heard a bang outside the public house followed by a man's cry. I ran out and saw Mrs. Ellis with a revolver. She was standing quite still with the revolver held loosely in her right hand and pointing at the dark haired young man I now knew to be Blakely who was lying face down on the pavement. He was moaning and blood was coming from his mouth.

The woman said, "Phone the police." He told her he was a police officer and took the gun from her. Later at the police station he found the revolver contained six spent cartridge cases, one in each chamber. It was in proper working order.

Continued on Page 7

*As with the Christofi case the previous year, this second killing in South Hill Park, Hampstead, attracted massive public interest. Article taken from the* Hampstead and Highgate Express, *27 April 1955.*

surrounding the hanging of Ellis for the crime was to become one of the most infamous and well-documented cases in modern British criminal and legal history and, still today, the crime continues to be vigorously debated by both the judiciary and the media.

Twenty-eight-year-old, Rhyl-born Ruth Ellis was different to Styllou Christofi in everyway but suffered the same ultimate fate. Despite taking a life, she was a woman brought up with a sense of morals and, as a result, accepted full responsibility for her foul deed. Believing in a 'life for a life', Ruth even wrote to the victim's mother explaining that she would accept her punishment without question or appeal. Her family and supporters maintained however, and continue to argue fifty years after her death, that her trial, and resulting sentence, was a gross miscarriage of justice. As recently as December 2003, three senior appeal judges threw out a posthumous appeal to overturn Ruth's murder conviction on the grounds that it was 'without merit'. The modern judiciary still felt adamant that Ruth Ellis was rightly convicted of murder under the law at the time of her court case. In a hearing lasting twenty minutes, Lord Justice Kay concluded:

*We have to question whether this exercise of considering an appeal so long after the event, when Mrs Ellis herself had consciously and deliberately chosen not to appeal at the time, is a sensible use of the limited resources of the court of appeal.*

The appeal was instigated by Ruth Ellis's sister, Muriel Jakubait, then aged eighty-one years. She and her legal team believed that her sister had suffered from 'battered woman syndrome' and requested that the murder conviction be quashed and substituted with a verdict of manslaughter.[31] In spite of the disappointing outcome to this appeal, Mrs Jakubait has vowed to fight on, declaring, 'I am never going to give up over this until I am taken from this earth.'

The crime itself was without complication. Quite simply, at around 9.30 pm on Easter Sunday, 10 April 1955, Ruth Ellis shot and killed her ex-boyfriend, twenty-five-year-old David Blakely, as he headed towards his car after emerging from the *Magdala Tavern*, South Hill Park. For good measure, as he lay wounded on the ground, she fired more three rounds into his body. One earlier shot ricocheted off a wall and hit the thumb of a passer-by, Gladys Kensington. Then, with the deed done, Ruth Ellis did not panic or try to escape but quietly surrendered to an off duty policeman drinking in the pub. In supporting Ellis's actions, many sympathisers believed that she was justified in seeking revenge for the physical and mental abuse inflicted upon her by Blakely during their brief but stormy relationship. To them, she was a woman driven over the edge.

As a divorced mother of two, platinum blonde Ruth made her way in the world from earnings she received as a nightclub hostess and part-time model. In 1953, due to her open and honest nature, she gained promotion to position of manager at *The Little Club*, a rather seedy drinking house in Knightsbridge. The situation afforded a comfortable

*The* Magdala Tavern, 2005. *Fifty years on the pub is still very much remembered for the shooting of David Blakely by Ruth Ellis.*

wage and free accommodation. It was here that she met David Blakely, a somewhat volatile young motor racing driver, and soon an intimate relationship developed. Ruth was mistakenly led to believe that the two might become engaged, during which time she even became pregnant but miscarried after Blakely had allegedly punched her in the stomach.

In spite of her social pretensions, Ruth soon realised that she would never be accepted into Blakely's family or social circle. Furthermore, she was to lose her job and flat as a result of Blakely's drunken behaviour at the club. Ruth found brief respite and a place to live with besotted, older businessman Desmond Cussen but, unbeknown to her benefactor, Ruth continued to liaise with her young racing driver. When Blakely complained about her arrangements with Cussen, she moved into a flat of her own at 44 Egerton Gardens, Kensington. As he began seeing other women, the driver soon tired of his relationship with Ruth and rejected her once and for all. Blakely then moved in with friends at 29 Tanza Road, Hampstead, only a short distance from

*David Blakely and Ruth Ellis in seemingly happier times.*

South Hill Park. Ruth was infuriated at his casual and insensitive manner towards her, especially made worse when he refused to see her or answer her telephone calls. Ruth became further incensed when she observed Blakely walking out with his Hampstead hosts' pretty young nanny. Now believing herself utterly betrayed, she acquired a loaded .38 Smith and Wesson revolver from an unidentified source – possibly Cussen – and, on 10 April, travelled to Hampstead with retribution in mind. On seeing Blakely's car parked outside the *Magdala Tavern*, Ruth waited for him to leave the premises before unleashing her terrible vengeance.

At her Old Bailey trial that began on 20 June 1955, Ruth made little attempt to defend herself. Even her defence counsel had trouble in persuading her to plead not guilty. But, she knew that she was responsible and so did the jury, who took a mere fourteen minutes to find her guilty of murder. Ruth rejected an appeal, and to the thousands who signed a petition to save her from the gallows she said, 'I am very grateful to them. But I am quite happy to die.' She was later refused a reprieve when the Home Secretary, Gwilyn Lloyd-George, announced that there were 'no sufficient grounds to recommend any interference with the due course of law.' And so, compliant with her wishes, prisoner 9656 Ruth Ellis was hanged by Albert Pierrepoint (his last) at 9 am on Wednesday, 13 July 1955 in Holloway Prison. Her execution incited intense protest and was to ultimately help in the fight to abolish capital punishment in this country. Even so, rather than for aiding judicial reform, Ruth Ellis will always be uniquely remembered for being 'the last woman to be hanged in Britain'.

# References

1. [C.C] 'The Legend of Mother Red Cap'. *North Middlesex and North Western Record.* November 1880.
2. Palmer, Samuel *History of St Pancras.* 1870, p. 257.
3. Collins, J.W (ed.) 'Mother Red Cap: copy of a letter from Henry Foxhall, Gentleman, to Charles Firebrace', *Esquire,* September 1666. J W Collins, 1843, pp 12–19.
4. Barrett, Thomas J. *The Annals of Hampstead.* Adam and Charles Black, 1912, p. 154.
5. ibid, pp 156.
6. Old Bailey Proceedings (OBP) Online (www.oldbaileyonline.org, 26 August 2004), July 1722, trial of John Morphew and Nathaniel Jackson (t17220704-24).
7. ibid, April 1721, trial of William Barton (t17210419-37).
8. ibid, January 1723, trial of Matthew Flood, John Levee and Richard Oakey. (t17230116-27).
9. ibid, June 1752, trial of Thomas Wilford (t17520652-31).
10. ibid, April 1771, trial of Richard Hewett and Benjamin Johnson (t17710410-29).
11. ibid, February 1786, trial of Joseph Rickards (t17860222-1).
12. ibid, December 1786, trial Michael Walker, Richard Payne and John Cox (t17861215-1).
13. Unidentified newspaper cutting, December 1786, held in 'Holborn Collection' (26:1 Crime) at Camden Local Studies and Archives Centre.
14. OBP, September 1745, trial of Edward and Deborah Lloyd (t17450911-40).
15. ibid, December 1717, trial of Jasper Arnold and William Goddard (t17171204-33).
16. ibid, October 1747, trial of Richard Henson (t17471014-21).
17. ibid, 1732, trial of John Adams (t17320705-5).
18. ibid, April 1750, trial of John Thrift (t17500425-29).
19. Walford, Edward. *Old and New London Vol. V.* Cassell, Petter and Galpin, [1897], p. 292.
20. Unidentified newspaper cutting, 3 October 1809, held in 'Heal Collection' (A IX 14) at Camden Local Studies and Archives Centre.
21. Unidentified facsimile, 'Duelling in Great Britain and Ireland' pp 224–234, held in 'Heal Collection' (A IX 17) at Camden Local Studies and Archives Centre.

22. *The Times*, 27 September 1815, p. 4.
23. Fido, Martin and Skinner, Keith *The Official Encyclopaedia of Scotland Yard.* Virgin Books, 1999, p. 106.
24. Unidentified newspaper cuttings, March–April 1845, held in 'Hampstead Collection' (H343) at Camden Local Studies and Archives Centre.
25. *The Times*, 25 September 1893, p. 9.
26. Channel 4 *The Last Secret of Dr Crippen* [Television documentary]. Broadcast Saturday, 17 July 2004, 8.00 pm – 9.00 pm.
27. Jackson, Robert *Coroner: The Biography of Sir Bentley Purchase.* Harrap,1963, p. 68.
28. Jones, Steve *When the Lights Went Down: Crime in Wartime.* Wicked Publications, 2000, p. 1.
29. ibid, p. 69.
30. *The Times*, 6 January 1949, p. 2 & 2 January 1951, p. 2.
31. Dyer, Clare *The Guardian*, 9 December 2003, p. 11.

# Bibliography and Further Reading

Brandon, David & Brooke, Adam *Tyburn: London's Fatal Tree*. Sutton Publishing, 2004.

Brown, Walter E. *The St Pancras Book of Dates of the Principal Events in the History of the Parish*. Metropolitan Borough of St Pancras, 1908.

Fido, Martin *Murder Guide to London*. Weidenfeld and Nicolson, 1986.

Gould, Robert and Waldren, Michael *London's Armed Police*. Arms and Armour Press, 1986.

Herber, Mark *Criminal London: A Pictorial History from Medieval Times to 1939*. Phillimore, 2002.

Hitchcock, Tim and Shoemaker, Robert, 'Old Bailey Courthouse', Old Bailey Proceedings Online (www.oldbaileyonline.org, 10 October 2004).

Lane, Brian *The Murder Club Guide to London*. Harrap, 1988.

Lovell, Percy & Marcham, W. *Survey of London Vol. XIX: Old St Pancras and Kentish Town*. 1938.

Marshall, Alan *The Strange Death of Edmund Godfrey: Plots and Politics in Restoration London*. Sutton Publishing, 1999.

Napley, Sir David *The Camden Town Murder*. Weidenfeld and Nicolson, 1987.

Pelham, Camden *The Chronicles of Crime or the New Newgate Calendar Vol. 1*. Reeves and Turner, 1886.

Thurston, Gavin *The Clerkenwell Riot: The Killing of Constable Culley*. Allen and Unwin, 1967.

# Index